In *Two Are Better Than One*, Greg and Julie Gorman present surprisingly fresh truths to make a difference in your marriage and life. If you want your marriage to live into the purpose God desires, read this book.

—Drs. Les & Leslie Parrott,
authors of *Saving Your Marriage Before It Starts*

Greg and Julie Gorman have written a classic in marriage books that brings a beautiful balance of timeless teachings from the world's top thought leaders and combines them with interactive scenes from our favorite Bible heroes. In *Two Are Better Than One*, Greg and Julie present fun, fresh and frank truths to lead you on a journey of significant discovery that will elevate your expectations and provide direction for your most precious earthly relationship—your marriage. Every couple will celebrate as they discover God's purpose for their marriage.

—Stephen Arterburn, Founder and Chairman of New Life Ministries; host of the #1 nationally syndicated Christian counseling talk show *New Life Live!*; host of New Life TV (tv.newlife.com); Founder of Women of Faith conferences; bestselling author

Two Are Better Than One is anchored in God's Word and packed full of insights and hope for a stronger and better love in marriage.

—Tim Clinton, EdD, author and President
of the American Association of Christian Counselors

God has afforded me to engage with thought leaders and content creators around the world. As I read *Two Are Better Than One*, I realized yet another personal benefit of a great book. Greg and Julie have done two great and unusual things in this book. They have demonstrated authenticity and vulnerability in every page. Secondly, they have given more than theory and ideas; they give practice and applicable tools to make your marriage better than ever.

—Mark Cole, CEO, John Maxwell Enterprise

This book is jam-packed with great ideas for renewing purpose, direction, and energy in your marriage! Whether you've been married for five or fifty years, Julie and Greg will walk you through creative ideas to generate discussion and new ideas with your spouse. Don't miss these great insights.

—Shaunti Feldhahn, social researcher, national speaker, and bestselling author of *For Women Only*

Hope, help, and healing. What keeps us from living out God's best purpose for our marriage? I believe we lose hope, we refuse help, and we sometimes doubt that healing is possible for us. And yet, God offers each of these to us because they're absolutely necessary in marriage. As you work your way through this book may you allow fresh hope to arise within you. May you be humble enough to receive the tangible help the Gormans offer here. And may you open your hands and ask God to heal your souls and make you whole. As you dare to draw near to each other and to God, you will know a fresh passion and purpose in your marriage that your souls have always longed for.

—Susie Larson, talk-radio host, national speaker, and author of *Your Beautiful Purpose*

We love the proactive passion, inspiring intentionality, and creative connecting of Greg and Julie Gorman. With their practical insights, *two* are *better* than one!

—Pam and Bill Farrel, codirectors of Lovewise, authors of 40 books, including the bestselling *Men Are Like Waffles, Women Are Like Spaghetti*

We will never drift into a great marriage. Greg and Julie Gorman help us know how to intentionally pursue a great marriage. This book does a great job of taking the timeless truth of Scripture and delivering a timely message for all couples. I encourage you to read this together as a couple. You'll be glad you did!

—Lance Witt, Founder, Replenish Ministries

Greg and Julie have a beautiful passion for helping others discover their unique purpose. They have paired this with their passion for helping married couples. I am looking forward to seeing how this book—and their ongoing work as LifePlan Facilitators—help others to discover their uniqueness and make their greatest contribution. As they say, that journey is not simply another task to complete but rather a celebration of who you are.

—David Mitchell, President, Paterson Center

Greg and Julie Gorman's approach to marriage is extremely practical, taking you on a step-by-step journey to strengthen your relationship. You'll discover the unique purpose of your marriage and learn how you and your spouse can pursue it together.

—Steve Gladen, Small Groups Pastor, Saddleback Church, author of *Small Groups With Purpose* and *Leading Small Groups With Purpose*

Do you want your marriage to be fruitful, to impact the kingdom of God? Are you unsure how to make this happen? Greg and Julie show you how to create your own marriage plan, and they offer a practical plan of their own that will inspire you as you go forward. Every page of this book provides marriage wisdom that is sage, sensitive, and scripturally sound. Get this book *now*!

—Dr. Peter and Lorraine Pintus, coauthors of *Intimacy Ignited*

Grounded in biblical truth, Greg and Julie Gorman reveal the full potential of God's richest blessings for marriages built on a strong foundation. In *Two Are Better Than One*, couples will receive practical insight into growing a more healthy and vibrant relationship. This book awakens us to pursue all that God intends for us in our marriages!

—Reid and Lisa Smith, Reid is Pastor of Discipleship, Christ Fellowship, gochristfellowship.com

Greg and Julie share invaluable ideas and practical ways to take marriage to a whole new level with rich meaning, and we love it!!! Take this journey, trust the process. You will be so glad you did! There is no better fortress than the one we build at home and this book will help you do just that.
—Scott M. Fay, Vice-President, John Maxwell Team

Two Are Better Than One is a fresh approach to what makes a great marriage. Whether you are a newlywed or have been married for decades, Greg and Julie Gorman will show you how to passionately pursue the purpose of your marriage together.
—David Alford, Pastor of Leadership Development, Saddleback Church

The word I think of to describe *Two Are Better Than One* is *intentional*. Julie and Greg have packed this book with practical ways to be intentional in making your marriage be the best it can be!
—Jill Savage, CEO of Hearts at Home, author of *Better Together*

Greg and Julie truly unlock the "power of two" in this highly practical book, encouraging every couple to discover just how rich their marriage can be. Their stories are raw and real, and the study guides at the end of each chapter help the readers apply the principles they outline. Whether you're a newlywed or celebrating fifty years, the Gormans can help you strengthen your marriage and fulfill your purpose.
—James Randall Robison, LIFE Today TV

Everything changes when your marriage isn't left to chance. Greg and Julie Gorman will help you do marriage on purpose. Packed with relatable stories, Scripture, and important questions, this book will guide you toward a happier home!
—Arlene Pellicane, author of *31 Days to a Happy Husband*

"Don't resign to live status quo ... Live your design" is the constant theme of this insightful resource. Anyone who is ready to discover God's purpose for their marriage will be delighted to walk through the pages of this book with Greg and Julie Gorman. *Two Are Better Than One* is a practical tool to help you build a NO-REGRETS MARRIAGE.

—Steve and Rhonda Stoppe, authors of *If My Husband Would Change I'd Be Happy & Other Myths Wives Believe*

Two Are Better Than One: Build Purpose and Unity in Your Marriage gives couples a down-to-earth, realistic way to evaluate their goals, desires and dreams. Greg and Julie not only share their personal experience, but also offer biblical insight into the purpose of two people bringing glory and honor to God through the union of marriage. This resource will help couples open up the lines of com- munication and move toward accomplishing the dreams and goals they have always wanted.

—Rob and Micah Maddox, Rob is Worship Pastor, Spotswood Baptist Church, Fredericksburg, Virginia

This may be the finest book on Christian marriage I have ever read. It is Bible-based, written to communicate truth, and helps us to understand our mate and ourselves like never before. Greg and Julie are clear: God has in mind your greatness, not just your goodness. But how can we live life like this? This book tells you how. Above all, this is a book about finding and becoming all that God intends for you. It tells you how to place yourself under His authority and truly live each moment of life hand-in-hand with God. Other than the Bible itself, you may never read another book so helpful in living His will for your life and His purpose for your marriage.

—Tom Paterson, author of *Living the Life You Were Meant to Live*, and creator of the LifePlanning process

Saying the word *marriage* can bring thoughts of anxiety and even failure for us. Marriage seems really hard; so many people have all but given up. But marriage is God's idea—He created it—for you! Greg and Julie Gorman introduce eye-opening concepts of what marriage can be, what God meant for it to be. Don't give up on the idea of marriage. Read this book and begin to understand that you CAN have a vibrant, fulfilling relationship!

—Matt Pilot, Stuart Campus Pastor, Christ Fellowship

Relatable. Real. Reassuring. *Two Are Better Than One* is much more than a good read. It's a guide for growing closer to one another and closer to God. Consider this book a tool to leaving a love legacy for generations to come and fulfilling your unique marriage purpose.

—Daphne V. Smith, Life Coach, speaker, and Retreat Facilitator for Well Done Life; also a certified member of the John Maxwell Team

One of the best books we've read on the topic of marriage! Greg and Julie give a blueprint for how to live out your marriage with passion and purpose. *Two Are Better Than One* is a refreshing reminder that God has a bigger design for your marriage than you might imagine.

—Steve and Becky Harling, Steve is the lead pastor at Foothills Community Church, and Becky is the author of *The 30-Day Praise Challenge*

In *Two Are Better Than One*, Greg and Julie Gorman will help you and your spouse identify your strengths, as well as the obstacles that are keeping you both from experiencing unity and like-mindedness in your marriage. With their coaching and helpful insights, you really can experience that two are better than one!

—Hugh and Cindi McMenamin, twenty-year veterans of pastoral ministry and coauthors of *When Couples Walk Together: 31 Days to a Closer Connection*

You will find heartfelt insight in this book as Greg and Julie share their struggles through their own marriage. We must realize that our differences as husband and wife actually make us better for each other. We can gain so much strength and learn to celebrate our marriage if we focus on living toward God's design for marriage, which is why you need to read this book.

—Brady and Pam Boyd, Brady is Senior Pastor of New Life Church in Colorado Springs, Colorado, and author of *Addicted to Busy*

When you ask 99 percent of people why they want to marry their mate or why they got married in the first place, their answer always has to do with compatibility. And that tells us that most people don't know why they SHOULD get married or what purpose their marriage should have. Greg and Julie have found a way to make every reader feel like they're sitting down for coffee with you and making marriage feel fun. Many married couples are working so hard to stay together, but without knowing the purpose of them getting together in the first place, they'll continually strive for a goal that leads them nowhere. *Two Are Better Than One* is for every relationship status. Whether you're single, dating, engaged, or married for 10 years and praying for a turnaround, this book will take your current or future marriage to the next level.

—Ryan Leak, author of *The One*

No matter what season you find your marriage in, this book will strengthen, refresh and encourage you to make your marriage all God intends it to be. Greg and Julie's authenticity into their marriage is courageous and so needed. They are iron for each other, sharpening each other in their quest to be better together. You will be challenged to examine your marriage in the light of God's Word. God intends for us to have a win-win in our marriage.

—Donna Fagerstrom, Prayer Coordinator for Speak Up/Carol Kent Ministry, speaker, women's ministry leader, and author

Two Are Better Than One ... It's more than a great biblical principle by which we should live our lives. It's also an amazing way to look at marriage. That's what Greg and Julie have done in their timely book; they've given us a fresh look at marriage. If you're looking for a resource with biblical principles and practical application exercises to not only strengthen your marriage but also give it a whole new purpose, then this book is for you. I'm looking forward to reading it again with my wife and applying the exercises together.
—Dr. George Powell, Founding Pastor, Abundant Life Church, Portland, Oregon, Founding Member, John Maxwell Team

The Gormans have done it again! With *Two Are Better Than One*, they have revealed one of the fundamental secrets of long happy marriages, and long happy lives, for that matter. By teaching and demonstrating how to focus on the blessings and positive, in stark contrast to the problem-solution paradigm, Julie and Greg have outlined a recipe for purposeful success in marriage and in life. As the "lesser half" of a happy thirty-year marriage myself, I found myself nodding and smiling at their lessons and examples. By the way, I learned a few things too!
—Ed DeCosta, Executive Coach, speaker, and author

Greg and Julie are a beautiful couple that walks the talk and helps transform couples and marriages by searching God's design and purpose through the work of the Holy Spirit.
—Todd and Jan Mozingo, founders of Revive Church, Stuart, Florida

Greg and Julie have hit it out of the park with guidelines for guaranteed success as a couple. Our seven-year marriage is proof positive that the thesis is true to the core!
—Tammy Maltby, author (tammymaltby.com),
and Jerry Melchisedeck Sr., Lt Col USAF (Ret),
licensed real estate broker, Colorado

Greg and Julie have great inspiration in their new book *Two Are Better Than One*. If you are looking to add value to your marriage, this is a God-inspired book that will change your life.
—Dan Cupp, Pastor, John Maxwell Certified Leadership Coach,
trainer, speaker, and nationally certified ReFocus Coach,
New Church Specialties

I have officiated many weddings over the years, and I have never met a couple who desired a marriage that was just average! When people get married, they are dreaming of a relationship that is meaningful and fulfilling. Yet, the majority of them end up settling for "just average." Greg and Julie Gorman's great book *Two Are Better Than One* provides practical tools and teaches you how to move way beyond average. Read this book, bring a reality check to your expectations, and develop a relationship that sets an example for others. Yes, marriage can be wonderful, but it will only happen when it is founded and guided by truth, trust, and effort to ensure each of you are living out the purpose for which God made you. I highly recommend this book to married couples, engaged couples, and individuals who are looking for a marriage partner. Great job, Greg and Julie! You are an example of what marriage can be!
—Danny Glover, coach, speaker, trainer, author, and the founder
and owner of Glover Consulting Services

My husband Bryan and I have been married for almost thirty years, while nearly all of our friends have gotten divorced. This broke our hearts and we knew we needed to do something. That's why we developed Leadership Starts at Home, an online Bible study for couples. When I stumbled across *Two Are Better Than One*, it confirmed those reasons. Too often, married couples continue to live their own lives, their own dreams, their own friends, and their own destinies, never taking into account that two really are better than one and that God puts us together for a reason. Maybe the reason is to work together or do ministry together. The truth is, while we might define ourselves by our workplace success, leadership truly starts at home. Greg and Julie nail that simple truth in this book. We'll be using it in our online studies for years to come.

—Tina Black, owner Paul Mitchell Schools,
John Maxwell leadership coach and speaker,
founder of online Marriage Bible Leadership Starts at Home

It's been quite a few years since I performed Greg and Julie's wedding ceremony. In the intervening years they have fought their share of battles, seen their share of success and amassed a rich storehouse of wisdom, tested in the furnace of real life. Working together in the high stress world of corporate sales, they learned not only to survive as a couple but to thrive! My pastor used to teach us this principle that I see so beautifully illustrated in Greg and Julie: "You can teach what you know, but you will reproduce what you are!" The principles in this tremendous book not only give us another theory on marriage, but for anyone willing to actually do what they have painstakingly laid out, they give a road map to the marriage you have probably been dreaming about! Greg and Julie are not just teaching us what they know; they are revealing what they are. I have absolutely no doubt that those of us who will follow their lead will be on our way to the quality of marriage they have. I have firsthand knowledge that suggests a marriage like theirs is the kind of marriage we all want!

—Gary Hay, Lead Pastor, Hope Church, Springfield, Missouri

Build Purpose and Unity in Your Marriage.

Greg + Julie Gorman

H22
PUBLISHING

H22 Publishing, Hobe Sound, Florida, USA

TWO ARE BETTER THAN ONE
Build Purpose and Unity in Your Marriage

Copyright © 2023 Greg and Julie Gorman

ISBN 978-1-9555-4655-3 (softcover)

All rights reserved. No part of this book may be reproduced in any form, except for brief quotations in printed reviews, without permission in writing from the publisher.

All Scripture quotations, unless otherwise indicated, are taken from the *Holy Bible, New International Version®, NIV®*. Copyright © 1973, 1978, 1984 by International Bible Society. Used by permission of Zondervan. All rights reserved.

Scriptures marked NKJV taken from the New King James Version®. Copyright © 1982 by Thomas Nelson. Used by permission. All rights reserved.

Printed in United States of America

CONTENTS

Acknowledgments 15

A Note from Greg and Julie 17

Chapter 1: What's the Big Idea? 21

Chapter 2: Are There Clues? 35

Chapter 3: Do You Live Problem Focused
or Purpose Focused? 53

Chapter 4: How Does God Confirm His Purpose? 69

Chapter 5: Why Are We So Different? 83

Chapter 6: What's Our Common Ground? 97

Chapter 7: What Fuels Our Purpose? 115

Chapter 8: How Do We Define Our Purpose? 131

Chapter 9: How Do We Protect God's Purpose? 149

Chapter 10: Now What? 165

About the Authors 183

Endnotes 185

ACKNOWLEDGMENTS

To our heavenly Father—thank You for the privilege of sharing Your message that is filled with so much life and purpose. Breathe Your life into this message, anoint it with Your Spirit, and accomplish all you intended for it to accomplish. We love You, Lord.

We want to express gratitude to the Paterson Center—Tom Paterson, Pete Richardson, and David Mitchell, may we continually impact lives to uncover God's specific design and build a legacy of purpose together.

To Dr. John C. Maxwell, the entire John Maxwell team of coaches and speakers—thank you for encouraging us to become all God intended for us to be. We are forever grateful for your friendship, belief, and support. May we continually influence others with our lives.

To our children, Courtney, Sommer, and Joshua—parenting you is among our greatest joys of life. May you always live the purpose God intended. May you, your spouses, your children, and your children's children continually enjoy a legacy of living purpose focused. We love you.

A NOTE FROM GREG AND JULIE

Dear friends,

Google estimates that over 129 million books exist in the world today—congrats and thanks for picking up this one. We're so glad you did and we know you won't be disappointed. After all, you're about to experience an incredible shift in the way you view your marriage.

So let's begin by saying that two really are better than one. No doubt you've heard that before, but you'll find the message contained in this book surprisingly fresh, fun, and frank. As a matter of fact, we've remained extremely zealous to only present truths we know will make a difference in your life and in your marriage. We won't try to convince you of anything; we'll simply deliver the evidence compiled from working with hundreds of couples over nearly two decades. So be ready to grow and be stretched.

As you read through the pages of this book, we'll lead you on a journey of significant discovery. We plan to stretch your thoughts and elevate your expectations concerning your most precious earthly relationship—your marriage. Both you and your spouse hold a distinct purpose together. God designed and destined your marriage for greatness. He hardwired your spouse and your DNA, combining them together with the intent of birthing something truly amazing—your marriage purpose. Though you probably have never considered that your marriage holds a specific purpose, and the thought of defining it may even seem a bit overwhelming, discovering your marriage purpose doesn't need to be complicated. In fact, we intend to show you just how simple it can be.

Along your journey, we'll share clues to help you discover your secret treasure, and we'll provide charts to help you safely navigate and stay on course during your voyage. Each chapter contains specific sections aimed to help you grow:

- A Timeless Truth to serve as a compass to point you in the right direction.
- A Discovery from God's Word and A Deeper Look at Scripture to provide strong anchors to keep you from drifting off course.
- Questions, Introspective Challenges, and Intentional Applications sprinkled throughout the chapters to personalize your journey and deepen your discovery.
- Thoughts from Leaders to bestow additional wisdom, insight, and breakthrough.
- We also transparently share our personal journey of discovery, as well as stories from other couples, to remind you that you aren't alone. In an effort to protect the privacy of friends, family, and coaching clients, however, names have been modified, but each story highlights true experiences from couples we've encountered throughout our marriage.
- At the end of each chapter, we've included a Study Guide filled with additional Questions, Scriptures, and Simple Prayers to enrich your communication and enhance your experience together.

We'd love to hear what you discover as the singular purpose for your marriage. You can connect with us by visiting our website at www.MarriedforaPurpose.com, where you'll also find valuable resources to encourage you in your marriage journey along with additional materials you can print to assist your discovery process.

A NOTE FROM GREG AND JULIE

Finally, we want to thank you for allowing us the privilege of journeying with you on this momentous voyage. Please know that we have prayed for you. We thoroughly believe God designed and destined you and your spouse for a specific purpose—that only the two of you can accomplish together. We can't wait for you to discover it. We believe with all our hearts that *Two Are Better Than One*.

Greg and Julie

Chapter 1

WHAT'S THE BIG IDEA?

A Timeless Truth
Couples who live for a greater purpose—
together—thrive.

Statistically, it has been suggested that 92–98 percent of evangelical believers struggle to identify their God-given purpose. With such a staggering statistic, it only stands to reason that the percentage for couples identifying their God-given purpose together must be even higher. After all, married life often intensifies our confusion. Kids, career struggles, and our everyday demands muddy the already murky waters of uncertainty. Living out an individual's purpose with clarity is tough enough, let alone combining it with another's. Yet God's big idea, His very purpose for your marriage, will be accomplished. He declares His plans from the very beginning and ensures they will be done.[1]

Get this. God has a purpose for you as an individual, and God has a purpose for your spouse. And when the two of you married, God designed a purpose for your marriage. Even better, you're about to discover that purpose.

Truthfully, we've always been the type of couple excited to move forward. We live to make a difference. We intentionally dedicate our life to helping others embrace their God-given design and become all He intended them to be as individuals, and also as couples. In saying that, it took quite a few years of self-development, thousands of hours of working with couples, and a ton of case studies to figure out why sometimes when couples did A and then B, they automatically experienced C, yet at other times when different couples faithfully did A and then B, the formula just didn't work out quite right.

After nearly two decades of observation, what we knew subconsciously but struggled to articulate finally presented itself. In the last several years, while working with couples, we stumbled across the catalyst causing some couples to thrive and others to merely survive (if that) in marriage. Since our discovery, we tested our newfound found truth and analyzed decades of observations. The more we reflected on our findings, the more God convinced us of His irrefutable insight—an insight that when *fully* embraced, by both husband and wife, will heal, restore, and deepen intimacy in every marriage.

Yes, in *every* marriage, no matter the condition of the relationship.

So what is it? What's the keen observation we identified that deepens connection and friendship in every marriage? What truth holds such promise? What's the catalyst promising so much confidence? We hope you're ready for it because we can't wait to share it. Couples who live for a greater purpose—together—thrive. They fundamentally understand that, unified in purpose, two are better than one.

Pretty simple, we know. But there's a huge difference between *simple* and *easy*. As our friend John Maxwell says, "Digging a six-foot hole is simple, but it ain't easy." Thus, we hope to ease the application of our discovery by providing insights, questions, and practical steps to help you reshape your rationale in order to reap the full benefits of its rewards in every facet of your relationship.

> A Thought from Rick Warren
> God deliberately shaped and formed you to serve him in a way that makes your ministry unique. He carefully mixed the DNA cocktail that created you.[2]

If you're like the majority of couples we work with, then you won't disagree that God holds a plan for you. Likewise, we're confident you'd acknowledge that God designed a plan for your spouse too. Yet you probably never considered the possibility that when you married, God devised a plan for you as a couple. If you're like most people, then you haven't spent a lot of time collectively uncovering or defining God's purpose for your marriage. No worries, because it isn't too late. God wants to reveal His plan for your marriage.

As a quick warning, you may be tempted to dismiss the magnitude of this simplicity, as its concept seems inconsequential; don't let its inconspicuous nature fool you. Your marriage purpose exerts extraordinary potential and remains a part of God's masterful plan dating all the way back to Adam and Eve.

A Discovery from God's Word

> Be fruitful and increase in number; fill the earth and subdue it.[3]

Awakening from his slumber, Adam opened his eyes to God's newest creation. Unlike any other created thing, Eve completed Adam. Her jaw-dropping beauty captivated his attention and aroused his curiosity. Her very essence incited a Pepé Le Pew-like response: "Wowza! Bone of my bone and flesh of my flesh. Hubba, hubba!" And with an infatuated Tarzan-like curiosity, Adam circled Eve, completely mesmerized by her design.

God chuckled, enjoying the completion of His creation. "C'mon, you two, let's walk together. I have a few things I'd like to show you." Hand in hand, Adam and Eve walked together—and with God—in the cool of the day. Everything seemed more brilliant, more alive. Adam swooned each time Eve spoke. Eve blushed every time Adam looked her direction. Together they felt fulfilled. Matched for eternity. Content. Satisfied. Electrified by one another's presence.

Pleased by their adoration for one another, God affectionately watched Adam and Eve. Everything transpired exactly as He'd planned—it was time for the big surprise, a surprise not only for them but a wonder that would echo throughout the ages.

"Adam! Eve! Look around. What do you see?"

Admiring God's handiwork, Adam and Eve shared their favorites. "I like the rugged lions with their powerful paws and kingly roars." Adam deepened his voice, trying to impress Eve. "I love how the magnolias elegantly adorn its branches." Eve sighed, reaching to place one of the flowers in her long midnight hair. Adam laughed out loud, losing all senses of his composure: "Whew! Eve's hot!"

Delighted by their response, God whispered, "It's yours. All of it."

Adam and Eve stopped midstep, amidst their midevening stroll. Like two wide-eyed children peering at a pile of gifts under a canopying Christmas tree, Adam and Eve looked on, amazed at the spectacular gifts God bestowed. Breathless, they soaked in the majesty of the moment, relishing God's creation for as far as their eyes could see.

"This is all for us?" Adam questioned.

Eve stuttered. "The fish? The birds? Every plant? They're... they're...they're all ours?"

"Yes!" God smiled. "I've entrusted all of creation to you. The bubbling brook is yours to enjoy. Every seed-bearing plant is yours to eat from (with only one exception). And every living creature is yours to rule."[4]

Excited and exhilarated, Adam and Eve pondered the extent of God's generosity. His intent for their life was magnificent, their every need masterfully provided for. Creation was at their fingertips.

Can you imagine Adam and Eve's thoughts? Everything they could ever dream of lay before them. But wait—the best was yet to come. Amidst their excitement, God whispered the next layer to His plan, the revelation of His big idea.

THE QUESTION
What is God's big idea?

> Then God said, "Let us make man in our image, in our likeness, and let them rule over the fish in the sea and the birds in the sky, over the livestock, over all the earth, and over the creatures that move along the ground."[5]

Did you catch it?

God's big idea is Adam and Eve.

And that plan hasn't changed. Since the beginning of time, God created man and woman to bear His image. He destined their union as the crowning jewel of His creation, saving the best for last. His invitation to "fill the earth and subdue it"[6] supplies the framework for every future generation and presents a prerequisite for accomplishment.

God's purpose for Adam and Eve's existence would only be completed if they fulfilled His assignment together. And since then, nothing's changed. The task of governing, ruling, and multiplying required Adam and Eve's interdependency—physically, emotionally, and spiritually—the same that is required of you with your spouse.

God's big idea lives on in you and your spouse.

Perhaps it's difficult for you to relate to Adam and Eve's seemingly perfectly matched, conflict-free relationship. As you think about their relationship, you find it easy to believe God holds a plan for a googly-eyed, head-over-heels in love kind of couple, but find yourself asking: "Purpose? How can God possibly have a purpose for *our* marriage? Sometimes, we wonder if God even intended us to marry one another. You have *no* idea of all the hardships we've encountered."

If so, then take courage. After all, lest we forget, Adam and Eve experienced their own set of difficulties and setbacks—remember the whole apple thing? They certainly didn't live problem-free. Thus, establishing our marriage purpose doesn't mean we live conflict-free, but we will live more united as we move forward toward a common purpose. Living God's purpose strengthens us to *become* all He intended us to be.

Maybe you look at the way God interacted with Adam and Eve and think, *We'd live out God's purpose too if He connected with us the way He did with them.* If so, hold up a moment. Doesn't God promise to walk with us?[7] To give wisdom to all who ask Him?[8] To secure a hope and a future for all of His children?[9] God promised that His Spirit would strongly support all who are completely His.[10] Don't miss this powerful truth here: God grants us the same opportunity for intimacy as He afforded to Adam and Eve. He desires for His children to interact with Him, to listen to Him, and to lay hold of His promises just as they did. Rest assured. God has always maintained a plan. And you and your spouse are a part of it.

Maybe you find yourself in a different group of couples who think, *Hmm. Purpose? I've never thought about a purpose for our marriage. We're all in, but we aren't the ministry type. Honestly, we're pretty simple. We're willing to be used, but can God hold a distinct purpose for a couple who doesn't feel called to a full-time ministry?* Oh boy, can He. Rest assured, because you and your spouse are His big idea.

Or, perhaps like most couples, you long to combine your passions and live with clarity, but the daily grind of getting the next thing done hinders you. It seems like your individual needs, along with everyone else's, become the object of your discussions and the focus of your disappointments. Instead of embracing God's specific design, His big idea, you find yourself looking at marriage and questioning, *There's a plan to all of this? We'd love to live God's design, but as it is we can barely keep our head above water. The best I can offer is taking care of my spouse's needs—and sometimes I fail at that.* If so, we get it! You aren't alone—take heart.

Discovering your purpose isn't another thing you need to do; it's more of a celebration of *who you are* as a couple. God's design for unity and purpose didn't end with Adam and Eve. He's created you and your spouse uniquely and holds a purpose for your marriage. Just like Adam and Eve, you and your spouse are His big idea.

> A Thought from Aristotle
> *The whole is greater than the sum of its parts.*[11]

God created you and your spouse for a work that only the two of you can accomplish together. He foresaw all your differences and carefully combined them together to complement one another. With great loving care, He fashioned you with common interests and instilled values to resonate with one another to make you one. With even greater care, God enmeshed and infused all of those qualities for His well-planned purpose. Why? Because together you will accomplish more than either of you could on your own. All throughout Scripture, God's Word permeates with the truth that together we are stronger. Let's take a deeper look.

A Deeper Look at Scripture

In Ecclesiastes 4:9–12, King Solomon wrote:

> Two are better than one,
> because they have a good return for their work:

> If one falls down,
> his friend can help him up.
> But pity the man who falls
> and has no one to help him up!
> Also, if two lie down together, they will keep warm.
> But how can one keep warm alone?
> Though one may be overpowered,
> two can defend themselves.
> A cord of three strands is not quickly broken.

And Jesus shares in the gospel of Matthew that "if two of you on earth agree about anything they ask for, it will be done for them by my Father in heaven."[12] And again, "where two or three have gathered together in my name, I am there in their midst."[13] Wow! What wonderful promises filled with so much hope!

Strong Together

Like most Christian couples, we wholeheartedly believe the soundness of God's Word. We don't question the Bible's authenticity or doubt its authority. Yet, when we first married, instead of embracing God's design and allowing His truth that together we are stronger to govern our relationship, we spent the first few years of marriage asserting our rights, demanding our way, and fighting to determine who would win. Instead of welcoming one another's strengths, we competed for control. We saw one another's differences as *opportunities* needing correction.

Boy, did we ever botch it up.

We spent the majority of our days trying to change one another to be what we thought we needed, and never considered the possibility that God designed us with distinct differences for a purpose. Our immaturity and ignorance stifled our ability to recognize or even consider God held a purpose for us as a couple. His big idea wasn't just a foreign concept; it was obsolete. Thankfully, God didn't abandon us to our oblivion. He healed our relationship by challenging us to love one another—unselfishly, unconditionally, and toward a unified purpose.

At first, He led our steps with warnings like "if you bite and devour one another, take care that you are not consumed by one another."[14] As we matured, He began guiding us with Scriptures offering positive affirmation to increase our expectation, like Ecclesiastes 4:12: "Though one may be overpowered, two can defend themselves. A cord of three strands is not quickly broken." God expanded our vision toward a common purpose. Instead of competing, we learned to celebrate one another's differences. Instead of assaulting one another's thinking, we appreciated one another's insights. As we grasped the truth that together we are stronger, we positioned our relationship to reap the benefits of working together, collectively, toward a common purpose.

> A Thought from Mother Teresa
> *I can do things you cannot, you can do things I cannot; together we can do great things.*[15]

Every marriage, unified in Christ, enjoys the hope expressed in Ecclesiastes 4—a good return, help, warmth, and strength. Together we defend more easily. Our alliance, with God at the center, remains complete, constant, and secure. The truth is that together two really are better than one.

Unity and Interdependency

Heather and Scott always wanted the best for one another. During their early years of marriage, Heather tirelessly worked two jobs to support Scott's education. Later in life, when Heather's mom took a turn for the worse, Scott secretly paid for all of her mother's medical costs. They share a strong commitment for family. If you ask them, blood runs thicker than water. Heather and Scott live to make God known through the evidence of their dedication to family.

Tom and Gina combined their strengths and formed a nonprofit ministry for sex-trafficked girls. Gina, the compassionate extrovert, extends counsel and a safe place to heal for each victim living in their safe house. Tom, the calculated businessman, lifts the weight of the organization's financial dealings and oversees all the state's legal requirements. They live for the common purpose of providing hope to the hopeless.

William winks at Mary, who can no longer open the jar of apple butter: "I'll open it if you'll put a little on my toast." Mary smiles, winking back to the fifty-year-old love of her life: "Deal." Their unified vision to reveal God's love by serving one another has stood the test of time.

And these couples aren't alone. They illustrate God's greater plan for unity and interdependency, as highlighted throughout Scripture. In Jeremiah 32:39, God promises the prophet that He'll give His people a singleness of heart. Later, in the Gospels, Jesus demonstrates that two are better than one by sending His disciples out two by two.[16] And in Acts 4:32, we witness the power of unity as believers come together to fast and pray. The result? Pentecost.

By now you may be asking, If God truly intended couples to accomplish more together than individually, then why do so many fail?

AN INTROSPECTIVE CHALLENGE
Shift your focus.

Unfortunately, like our early years of marriage, many couples get stuck focusing their attention on their differences. They concentrate on overcoming their issues and tryiing to fix their problems. If that's you, we hope to shift your focus to God's big idea.

Couples who enjoy marriage and celebrate their relationship to its fullest focus their energy toward living a unified purpose. They understand that significance and fulfillment flourish when they live out God's design for their marriage.

Over the next several chapters we'll lead you on an awesome treasure hunt by providing insights, questions, and hands-on resources to help you and your spouse shift your focus to your marriage purpose.

AN INTENTIONAL APPLICATION
Invite God to reveal His purpose for your marriage.

Remember, you are God's masterpiece.[17] He created you distinctly, on purpose and for a purpose. He hardwired your DNA and gifted you with everything you need pertaining to life and godliness.[18] Likewise, He lovingly and masterfully created your spouse.[19] He crafted your personalities, internally wiring them to complement and complete one another.[20] When you married, God fashioned a purpose for your union and intended for you to fight to protect it at all costs.[21] Together you're a powerful force. You're stronger because you're together.[22] Your unified passions, when aligned with God's, are simply unstoppable.[23]

Study Guide: Chapter 1

For an expanded study and in preparation for upcoming chapters, take a moment to share your thoughts with one another through the following section. Each study guide presents questions to promote quality conversations to facilitate your discovery process. Reading this book will not reveal your marriage purpose—participating and applying the concepts and exercises will.

As you reflect on the following questions and Bible passages, and then intentionally connect with one another through prayer, remember to keep your conversations positive. Take responsibility for your own actions. After all, as the host of the number one nationally syndicated Christian counseling talk show *New Life Live*, Stephen Arterburn shares, "The more responsibility you take for your choices, the less regret they're likely to cause you."[24] Be accountable. Look for opportunities to build up your partner and to dream together. Invite God to reveal His purpose for your marriage.

Questions to Consider

1. Reread Ecclesiastes 4:9–12 and envision living it. Begin asking one another, How can we live God's purpose in our marriage?

2. Proverbs 27:17 says, "As iron sharpens iron, so one person sharpens another." Take a moment to express in positive terms how you help one another grow. (Remember, as you share with one another, be intentional about building up one another with your words.)

3. What potential dangers or risks could sabotage your process of discovery? (For example, unforgiveness, busyness, fatigue, comfort, routine, etc.)

4. What ground rules can the two of you establish together to protect your marriage from those risks? (For example, take accountability for your own actions instead of pointing out how your spouse needs to improve.)

5. Do you have mutual friends who want to strengthen their marriage and would benefit from discovering their purpose? If so, then consider studying this book with them to provide additional support and accountability.[25]

Scriptures to Study

- Genesis 1:26–29; 2:18
- Deuteronomy 32:30
- Ecclesiastes 4:9–12
- Proverbs 29:18
- Matthew 19:5–6; 28:19–20
- Romans 12:6
- Ephesians 2:10
- 2 Peter 1:3

Prayer invites the limitless power of God to do in a single moment what we could never accomplish if given a lifetime. No matter your circumstances, no matter the years of no return, no matter the condition of your relationship, *never* give up. In a simple touch, in one single encounter, the God who breathed stars into existence and fashioned the entire world by His spoken word, does the miraculous. Take a moment to invite His presence, wisdom, and purpose to be revealed in your marriage. Make prayer a part of your discovery process and everyday living.

Study Guide: Chapter 1

A Simple Prayer

Father, we realize we have nothing to give You except what You have already given to us. Yet we gladly extend all we possess (our gifts, our talents, and our relationship) as an expression of our love back to You. Grant us strength, wisdom, and unity to accomplish Your purpose for our marriage. Reveal Your plan for our marriage and then help us to live it out as one. Amen.

Chapter 2

ARE THERE CLUES?

A Timeless Truth
The foundations for our marriage purpose
must be established by God and for God.

As kids we both possessed a bent toward being detectives. Julie read every book in the Nancy Drew Mystery series and Greg—well, secret be told—Greg always held a deep desire to be Underdog: "Never fear, Underdog is here!"[1] Our aspirations to help the distressed, solve a good mystery, and capture the villain didn't turn out exactly as we first envisioned, but in many ways they carried with us into marriage. Today, we love helping those who seek understanding, stopping the Enemy from killing, steal- ing, and destroying, and sharing clues to solve one of the greatest mysteries a couple could hope to unravel: Why do we exist? What's our collective purpose? And what is God's plan for our marriage? As we voyage forward together on the quest of discovering your hidden treasure, we want to encourage you: You aren't alone in this journey. Lots of exciting discoveries await you. But for now, take a deep breath. Relax. And, for a few moments, suspend the grandiose idea your marriage holds a *single* purpose. Though you will (if you faithfully participate in each exercise of this book) discover the purpose for your marriage, for now we invite you to simply look for the clues and to consider the possibilities. There are no wrong answers here—just a treasure hunt leading you closer to the booty. (For the record, *booty* is a term pirates used for treasure, although Greg likes to think of the term otherwise.)

Okay, now that you're not taking yourself too seriously, we encourage you to enjoy the voyage you're about to embark on together. Andy Stanley once said, "Direction not intention determines our end destination."[2] That said, direction and intention go hand in hand. In fact, in order to gain clear direction, we must first maintain a specific intention or purpose for our direction. The purpose is, in fact, what determines the direction, isn't it?

Throughout this next chapter you'll uncover three clues that provide a framework for your marriage purpose. Each clue reveals a principle that is necessary for building a strong, unified marriage purpose. Don't get in a rush. Don't be overwhelmed. Remember, God always provides all that you need, to do all that He's called you to do—a principle Nehemiah learned around 444 BC.

A Discovery from God's Word

"The God of heaven will give us success. We his servants will start rebuilding...."[3]

Nehemiah held his hand over his fluttering heart and reminded himself: *This is big, but God is bigger.* Judah's walls had been destroyed and God's people remained scattered all across the land. God commissioned Nehemiah to the seemingly impossible task of rebuilding Judah's border from remnants lying in ruins for over a hundred years.

The next morning, Nehemiah's words flowed effortlessly as he stood before the king and queen: "If it pleases the king and if your servant has found favor in his sight, let him send me to the city in Judah where my fathers are buried so that I can rebuild it."[4]

ARE THERE CLUES?

The king looked to the queen, who always ruled by his side. Without hesitation, the corner of her lips turned to a half grin as she tilted her head slightly to affirm what the king was about to do. "How long will your journey take, and when will you get back?"[5] he asked.

Nehemiah beamed. Filled with faith at the king and queen's support and consent, he quickly devised a plan for his journey and set off toward his homeland. It wouldn't take long for him to reach Judah's border, nor for the faith that had just surged within him to feel challenged.

"Oh, Lord, how can this be? It's worse than I imagined." Nehemiah looked out in disbelief—Judah's wall was obliterated—only rocks, burnt stones, and massive debris remained. Fragments of a once elaborate fortress reduced to rubble, chippings, and pebbles of gravel scattered across the land. Nehemiah wept bitterly as he lowered his head to the ground. "Oh, God, who am I that I should be called to rebuild this wall? It's impossible."

Perhaps similar thoughts cross your mind at times too. You find yourself thinking, *Who are we that we should be called to do something for God? You obviously don't know our past. Apparently you didn't realize that we are just average, ordinary, everyday people.* Or maybe you've even voiced your feelings to God: *This feels impossible! We're not strong enough. We're not smart enough.* If so, trust us—we completely understand.

During some of our most difficult seasons, we have felt the same way. When we considered God's purpose and the tasks He called us to, we thought, *This is impossible! We can never do that.* But do you want to know a secret? Every couple called to make a difference feels similar feelings until they remember God's still in control.

Suddenly, a familiar presence flowed through Nehemiah's thoughts and offered comfort to his soul: *Wait, Nehemiah. Look again. Take stock of your resources. The massive stones that once built these walls lay before you, unmoved. My people, once arrogant but now humbled, are ready to rebuild. Everything you need waits at your feet.*

Encouraged and inspired, Nehemiah reopened his eyes. Instead of rubble, he envisioned resources. Instead of defeat, he remembered Israel was meant to rule, not to be ruled. Instead of burnt stones, Nehemiah noticed foundations, primed and ready to be built upon. And the same stands true for you too.

Husbands, wives, open up your eyes; see the hope set before you. Remember that you are God's big idea. Your marriage holds purpose. You were meant to rule, not to be ruled. The circumstances that brought you to where you are today simply served as the process (God chose) to lead you to where He is taking you. Though you may feel humbled, the refining process prepared you for the very purpose God designed for your marriage. So rest assured, His purpose will be established. Though the Enemy has attempted to desecrate God's design for marriage, beneath all the rubble are foundations ready to be built upon. Your marriage is firmly founded in Christ, planned and blessed by God Himself. And like Nehemiah and Nehemiah's countrymen, God empowered and entrusted something special for you to do, a purpose only you and your spouse will accomplish together.

Nehemiah turned once more to survey the landscape, pausing before the massive amount of work. "Looks like it's time to gather help," he said. In a loud, booming voice, he rallied his countrymen: "C'mon, men. Start where you are! Shards, rocks, boulders—fill it all in; use what you have."

And every man did just that. In fifty-two short days, the people rebuilt Jerusalem's walls and one hundred years of desolation reached its end. Why? Because God's people worked together as one. Each family participated in rebuilding the area around them. As they worked together, they accomplished what others thought impossible. Do you see how direction and applied intention determined Nehemiah's end destination?

Now it's your turn.

Let's sift through the resource of God's Word to uncover the three overarching principles establishing a firm foundation for your marriage purpose: *C'mon, men and women (husbands and wives), start where you are. Use what you have. Rebuild your walls. You possess everything you need to do all God purposed you to do.*

Three Overarching Principles to Secure Your Marriage Purpose

Before diving in to identify your precise marriage purpose, don't overlook these three fundamental principles. They secure the essential foundation to building a sustainable purpose. The final sturdiness and condition of any building, whether a home or skyscraper, is directly impacted by the stability of its foundation. A weak foundation causes the whole structure to be compromised, from bottom to top. A strong foundation, however, reinforces a sturdy platform and determines how tall the tower can stand and how strong a storm it can withstand.

The same applies for any area of life, whether our family relationships, health, finances, business, or even marriage purpose. We need sturdy foundations to sustain long-lasting results. Thus, foundations are necessary to build anything of quality. When winds blow and storms come, the foundation of a building determines the security of its structure.

Jesus said it this way:

> "Therefore everyone who hears these words of mine and puts them into practice is like a wise man who built his house on the rock. The rain came down, the streams rose, and the winds blew and beat against

that house; yet it did not fall, because it had its foundation on the rock...."[6]

Let's build our marriage purpose on the unshakable foundation of Christ Himself and God's Word.

> **A Thought from R. A. Torrey**
> We live in an age of hustle and bustle, of man's efforts and man's determination, of man's confidence in himself and in his own power to achieve things, an age of human organization, human machinery, human scheming, and human achievement. In the things of God, this means no real achievement at all.[7]

At the very outset, it's important to remember that the foundations for our marriage purpose must be established *by* God and *for* God. Human ingenuity is a sad substitute for godly wisdom. Creativity, though powerful, will only get us so far. Determination and dedication are necessary, but even the greatest warriors grow weary. Thus, lasting foundations must be built upon the eternal truths founded in God's Word. So let's get started.

Principle One: Live the Great Commission

Before you roll your eyes and say, "Tell us something we don't know," remember strong towers require deep, steady foundations. As believers, our primary task is to make Jesus known. Even if you aren't the "ministry type," there is no such thing as a Christian without a calling; likewise, there is no such thing as a marriage without a ministry. God hardwired it into our DNA. He designed us with the desire to be part of something greater than ourselves and commissioned us to be a light in our homes,[8] to share the good news,[9] and to bear lasting fruit.[10] God sends us just as He sent His Son.[11]

What does living the Great Commission look like in our modern world? Complex. Vast. Expansive.

> A Thought from Rick Warren
> *You were born by his purpose and for his purpose.*[12]

Our method of living the Great Commission takes on a variety of forms within the context of marriage. As a matter of fact, our God-given gifts and callings are as unique as God is creative. In *Living the Life You Were Meant to Live,* Tom Paterson, creator of the proven LifePlanning process, writes, "Your unique giftedness points toward your unique purpose. God has given you gifts to use, and when you use your gifts, you fulfill your purpose in life."[13] As a couple, you might make God known by serving people in your community or serving people overseas. Making Him known may play out in raising godly children or by serving aging parents. You may reveal His love by serving in the children's ministry at your local church or by building a business that honors Him in the workplace. Making Him known isn't an item on an exhaustive to-do list; rather, making Him known plays out in every fiber of your being and flows from the depths of your design. After all, we are *human beings,* not *human doings.*

Living the Great Commission isn't so much in *what we do* but in *who we are.* Your gifts make up who you are. And, as a couple, God already designed and innately equipped you with gifts and passions that make you and your spouse uniquely who you are. It's who you are as a couple and the activities bringing forth life *to you* and *from you* that point you more clearly toward God's purpose for your marriage. A great question to consider asking is, How do we (most naturally) make God known right where we are?

> A Thought from Bill and Pam Farrel
> *Your unique ability forms a treasure in you that was designed to make a difference in the world.*[14]

Keep in mind that you don't need to be famous, celebrated, or world renowned to make a difference—you're significant because God already chose you and equipped you and your spouse for a purpose. In the New Testament, God chose tax collectors,[15] fishermen,[16] and uneducated people[17] to establish the foundation of the church as we know it. In doing so, God demonstrates that He chooses whomever He wishes and qualifies whomever He's chosen. Make no mistake about it: you've been chosen. Gain courage by simply welcoming your design and recognizing that God is the giver of gifts.[18] The expression of His gift, in and of itself, then, is merely the megaphone or amplifier of making Him known through your marriage. In Romans, Paul writes it this way:

> We have different gifts, according to the grace given us. If a man's gift is prophesying, let him use it in proportion to his faith. If it is serving, let him serve; if it is teaching, let him teach; if it is encouraging, let him encourage; if it is contributing to the needs of others, let him give generously; if it is leadership, let him govern diligently; if it is showing mercy, let him do it cheerfully.[19]

THE QUESTION
How can we live the Great Commission by utilizing our specific gifts?

God has designed you and your spouse on purpose and for a purpose. He entrusted you with a mission to make Him known and commissioned you to begin that process within your own marriage and in your home. In Matthew, Jesus said, "You are the light of the world. A city on a hill cannot be hidden. Neither do people light a lamp and put it under a bowl. Instead they put it on its stand, and it gives light to everyone in the house."[20] Did you catch the correlation and the undeniable application within this passage?

Our light should first provide light for the members of our own household. In other words, sometimes we look for an outside expression to make God known when the greatest opportunity to reveal Him lies right beneath our nose and underneath our rooftop. When we make Him known there, in the home, we compound our ability and expand our influence to reach the world. We must get it right there first. Why? Because we reveal who we really are behind the closed doors of our homes. How we respond, how we interact with our family, and how we speak to our spouse and children offers the clearest indication of our heart's condition. If we want to leave a lasting legacy and to live a life of significance, we need to begin living God's purpose within the walls of our home. Your marriage purpose will always bring life to one another and to your family first. If not, then you may need to reevaluate if your desires are misplaced or rooted in wrong motives.

As you search to define your marriage purpose, remember to begin where you are and consider some important questions: How can our distinct passions and purpose first bring life to our family? Does our marriage purpose add value to one another and reveal Christ to our family? How can we (best) make God known in our marriage, to our children, and then to our world?

Principle Two: We Were Created to Bring God Pleasure[21]

In *The Practice of the Presence,* Brother Lawrence writes, "Our sole occupation in life is to please God."[22] Wow! Can you imagine how different our world would be if our only ambition as married couples was to bring God pleasure? If our sole occupation was to bring Him delight? Can you imagine how different our lives would be if every activity we engaged in was to bring God joy and cause Him to smile?

In the movie *Chariots of Fire*, Eric Liddell was quoted as saying: "I believe God made me for a purpose, but he also made me fast! And when I run I feel His pleasure."[23] When we embrace God's design for our marriage purpose, it makes God smile, and when we live His purpose together, it brings Him pleasure.

A Deeper Look at Scripture

Scripture says, "For from him and through him and to him are all things."[24] Our purpose came *from* God and is upheld *through* Him. Discovering our marriage purpose and then offering it back *to* Him is a spiritual act of worship. Our marriage brings God pleasure when we extend our gifts back to Him, for His service, and live according to the purpose He designed for our marriage. In Philippians 2, Paul shares an extensive list on how we bring God pleasure. He writes that we are to

- be of the same mind,
- maintain the same love,
- live united in spirit,
- focus intently on one purpose,
- do nothing selfishly or conceitedly,
- and humbly regard one another as more important than ourselves.

Don't mistake Paul's invitation here. We would be remiss if we approached Paul's instructions with a now-I've-got-to-do-this attitude. Instead, look at Paul's invitation in its entirety as he writes:

> If you have any encouragement from being united with Christ, if any comfort from his love, if any fellowship with the Spirit, if any tenderness and compassion, then make my joy complete by being like-minded, having the same love, being one in spirit and purpose. Do nothing out of selfish ambition or vain conceit,

but in humility consider others better than yourselves. Each of you should look not only to your own interests, but also to the interests of others.[25]

Eureka! What is Paul saying here? Did you capture his full invitation?

Instead of approaching life with a here's-one-more-thing-we-gotta-do, now-we-have-to-serve-one-another-unselfishly kind of attitude, look at the real invitation being expressed. Paul encourages us to be like-minded, to maintain the same love, and to be one in spirit; his invitation is to live purpose focused. When we live purpose focused, our relationship and servanthood is *not* drudgery—it's life giving and it brings forth joy.

When we fully embrace this passage, to live united with our spouse in purpose, we can't help but celebrate life together. Embracing a cohesive purpose and living intentionally to fulfill it results in a unified life, where we experience laughter, joy, and have fun together. And our contribution as a couple is inevitable.

A Thought from Dale Carnegie
People rarely succeed unless they have fun in what they are doing.[26]

When we grab hold of God's big idea for our relationship—that two are better than one—then we model our life after Christ Jesus who lived to fulfill the Father's purpose. Our unity reflects the cooperative nature of the Trinity and brings God pleasure. As we bring God pleasure, we perpetuate more of Him in our relationship, and the more we perpetuate Him in our relationship, the more we live life as He intended.

The result of living toward a common purpose causes us to serve one another more naturally. This is because we share the same mind-set as we move forward together, to live out God's design. Inevitably, when we shift our thinking to His purpose, we shift our thinking from, *How can I get my spouse to change?* to *How can we accomplish His purpose together?* Instead of comparing and competing to get our needs met, we begin living intentionally to accomplish the same purpose. Instead of trying to implement a bunch of dos and don'ts, we govern our actions with questions like, God, how can we bring You pleasure in our marriage? How can we impact this world together?

AN INTROSPECTIVE CHALLENGE
How can we best bring God pleasure?

Friends, God's purpose lives in you. As you search for your marriage purpose, allow His overarching qualifier of bringing Him pleasure to govern the specifics of your marriage purpose. When you immerse your combined skills and passions in a pursuit of bringing God pleasure and temper your gifts with His unconditional love, then you will build a secure foundation to live a unified marriage purpose.

> A Thought from Stephen Arterburn
> *[Our] highest purpose as humans and followers of Jesus—is to be a conduit of God's love.*[27]

Principle Three: God Designed Marriage to Demonstrate His Unconditional Love

When we first married, unconditional love seemed like an impossible concept. We both reserved our love, with conditions. Julie struggled with insecurities, stemming from earlier childhood abuse. It took years to unravel her unspoken vows of *I'll never let another man hurt me* and *I won't ever feel vulnerable again.* Likewise, Greg conditioned his love with qualifiers of *I won't be controlled by anyone* and *no one's going to tell me how to live.*

As you might imagine, our unexpressed needs eventually escalated to shouting matches of demanding our rights. Our individual mandates obstructed our ability to express love unconditionally. Yet one of the greatest invitations God extends to married couples is to love as He has loved us.[28] Marriage especially affords us with the opportunity to practice that command. If we want to build a strong legacy and live the purpose God designed for us as couples, then we need to build upon the foundation of unconditional love. Our demonstration of unconditional love serves as the greatest megaphone possible. God's unconditional love extends a rare gift in a world filled with conditions.

Think about it for a moment. When we extend grace and avoid saying derogatory comments about our spouse, people want to know why our relationship stands so strong. When we serve one another in desperate situations, faithfully and without resentment, people want to know what makes us so different.

In his book *Replenish,* our friend Lance Witte writes, "There's a huge difference between being a son/daughter and being an employee. A company has a transactional relationship with the employee. You produce…you're in. You don't produce…you're out. Your compensation is connected to your contribution. But it's different being a son or daughter. You are family. Your place is not dependent on your performance. As a son (daughter), my value is intrinsic, not transactional."[29]

When we build a marriage purpose centered on God's unconditional love, we serve as a living example of His love for the church and secure the foundations of His purpose for our marriage. All throughout Scripture, God uses the love shared between husbands and wives to illustrate His love for the church.

- In the Old Testament, God commands Hosea to marry the prostitute Gomer. He uses Hosea's story to serve as an illustration of His relentless and unconditional love for His people.
- In Ephesians, God shares that a man will leave his father and mother and become one with his wife, and then He compares it to the mystery of Christ and the church.[30]
- In Revelation, we see illustrations of the bride preparing herself for the wedding feast.[31] How does a bride prepare herself? Reluctantly? Begrudgingly? With indifference? No way! A bride wants to be found beautiful. She does everything possible to make her appearance beautiful, eagerly anticipating seeing her groom.

God designed us to uphold this same attitude toward Him and toward our spouse.

> **A Thought from Shannon Ethridge**
> *God intended the marriage relationship to be a reflection of His relationship to us—a relationship that remains steadfast because it isn't based on fickle feelings or human worthiness but rather is based on uncompromising commitment.*[32]

Marriage affords us with an unmatched opportunity to model God's love. By design, if we allow Him, we gain a greater understanding of His love for us as He equips us and extends His love through us to our spouse. Serving one another provides the final overarching principle to govern the details of our marriage purpose.

AN INTENTIONAL APPLICATION

Invite God to reveal how He desires for you to make Him known, bring Him pleasure, and demonstrate His unconditional love.

If it feels a little muddy, don't worry. You've made a lot of progress so far. You've moved a considerable amount of debris and uncovered three foundational principles that are essential in shaping how you construct your marriage purpose. Your specific marriage purpose will

1. make God known,
2. bring God pleasure, and
3. demonstrate His unconditional love.

In our next chapter, we'll build upon these three fundamental foundations by laying a little more groundwork to ensure our focus and attitude remain positioned in the proper place. But before you continue your voyage to discover the treasure of your marriage purpose, take a moment to reflect on the following questions, providing additional insights for connection.

Study Guide: Chapter 2

You're now equipped with three principles to serve as a foundation to build your marriage purpose:

1. Make God known.
2. Bring God pleasure.
3. Demonstrate His unconditional love.

Take a few minutes to consider the following questions as you move forward to uncover God's purpose for your marriage.

Questions to Consider

Ask one another each of these questions:

1. How can we better make Jesus known in our home, our community, and our church?
2. How is our marriage currently pleasing God? What are we doing well? Where do we need to grow?
3. What are some simple ways we can demonstrate God's unconditional love every day in our actions and in the way we speak to one another?

Scriptures to Study

- Matthew 4:18–20; 5:14–16; 10:3; 11:25; 28:19
- Mark 16:15
- Luke 24:47–48
- John 15:16; 20:21

Study Guide: Chapter 2

- Romans 12:6–8
- Ephesians 4:8–13; 5:31–32
- Philippians 2:1–4
- Colossians 1:16; 3:17–23
- Revelation 4:11; 19:7

A Simple Prayer

Father, we long to know Your distinct purpose for our marriage. We want to say yes to all You've planned for us. As we move closer to discovering our marriage purpose, please continually remind us that our purpose will make You known, will bring You pleasure, and, most of all, will reveal Your love. Help us to live those overarching purposes every day of our lives. In Your name we pray, amen.

Chapter 3

DO YOU LIVE PROBLEM FOCUSED OR PURPOSE FOCUSED?

A Timeless Truth
You find what you are looking for.

Thought leaders from Baptists to Buddhists agree on one central truth (though expressed in a variety of ways): We become what we think about, we get what we expect, and we find what we are looking for. Our thoughts hold power, they impact our results, and they shape our outcome. Our thoughts influence our relationships and control how we interact with others. They affect who we become.

King Solomon, the wisest dude who ever sported a pair of flip flops, said it this way: "As a man thinks in his heart, so he is."[1] The key is to take this profound revelation and apply it to our every day by governing what we entertain and controlling our thoughts. Though it may seem like a self-improvement mind game, in actuality it's God's invitation to a higher level of thinking and a shift in your focus.

Stay with us for a moment and consider the weight of this truth. If King Solomon and every other thought leader is right, that we become what we think about and that our outcome begins in our mind-set, then if we constantly focus on our issues we unwittingly perpetuate the subject of our thoughts, which is the problem. However, if we harness our thinking to align with God's, embracing the truth that we are created on purpose for a purpose, we reap the benefits of living fully and powerfully in the design He destined for our lives and marriage.

> A Thought from Napoleon Hill
> *Every man is what he is, because of the dominating thoughts which he permits to occupy his mind.*[2]

In his book *Good to Great*, Jim Collins and his team collected a total of ten and a half people years of research.[3] After scores and scores of studying good-to-great companies, alongside of comparison companies, Jim writes, "Greatness is not a function of circumstance. Greatness, it turns out, is largely a matter of conscious choice."[4]

Greatness is a matter of choice; we truly become what we think about and we create what we envision. Our focus largely determines what we produce. Think about it: Artists create masterpieces gathered from their ability to envision their end product, and athletes win medals largely determined by mental strength. David faced Goliath, not by matching brute strength with brute strength, but by the shift in his thinking. His focus clearly determined his victory.

A Discovery from God's Word

> You come against me with sword and spear and javelin, but I come against you in the name of the Lord Almighty, the God of the armies of Israel, whom you have defied.[5]

The morning began like the last thirty-nine. For forty days, Goliath hurled insults defying Israel. With a snakelike sneer and a gut-curling laugh, Goliath jabbed and jeered, invoking Israel to war: "C'mon and fight me, you pathetic, sniveling, circumcised weaklings! I'll tie one hand behind my back, wear a blindfold, and still plunder your treasures by midday. Is there no man among you?"

We can't go on like this, Saul thought, pacing back and forth. "Who'll go to war against this monstrosity?" Suddenly, Saul stopped wringing his hands: "Wait! I've got an idea to incite a hero." His declaration quickly scurried throughout the camp to everyone except the ruddy teenager, David. David had other things on his mind: an urgent message from his father.

"Eliab! There you are," David exclaimed. "How are we doing?" In typical fashion Eliab turned away, annoyed by David's presence.

Unbothered, David ran to greet his next two eldest brothers. "Abinadab! Shammah! Father said to tell you..." But before David finished his sentence, the Philistine champion from Gath shouted another taunt.

David thought to himself, *Who does this guy think he is? Why hasn't someone shut up his foul mouth?* Then David demanded, "Somebody, please tell me what's going on!" Though David's stature paled in comparison to the average Israelite, something about his tenacity intrigued a small crowd of Israelites. A short, stubby soldier piped up: "Do you see that big dude? Every day he challenges Israel. The king promised great wealth, exemption from taxes, plus his daughter's hand in marriage to the man who kills him."[6]

David looked at Goliath still spitting and frothing at the mouth, his frayed dreadlocks and razorlike fangs reminding David of the lion he'd fought last week. "Run that by me one more time." Then he thought, *You've gotta be joking; I'll do that for free!*

David rejected the conventional wisdom of swords and shields, passing them up for his trusted shepherd's weapon: "Five smooth stones and a sling ought to do the trick." David defied Goliath's insults, shouting back, "You come to me with a sword, with a spear, and with a javelin. But I come to you in the name of the Lord of hosts, the God of the armies of Israel, whom you have defied."[7]

What was David's defining difference? Surely he recognized the weapons formed against him, right? Surely David saw Goliath's size, sword, and spear. Goliath was big, mean, and ugly. The difference wasn't what David didn't see, but in where he placed his focus. While others contemplated their defense, David took the offense. While Israel's most valiant warriors cowered, cringing, feeling helpless and defenseless against Goliath's superior swordsmanship and brute strength, Goliath's nine-foot-nine-inch stature never deterred David. Instead, David focused on God and Goliath was no match for Him.

Sure, Goliath was big, but not big enough. Sure, the giant caused men to shake in the natural, but his size was no challenge to the Living God. Put side by side, Goliath was a small speck, a tiny flea, an inconsequential little pimple compared to the Breather of stars, Designer of galaxies, and Creator of time itself. Undaunted, David set out to decapitate the abomination who dared to defy his family, his countrymen, and most importantly His God. While others saw the problem, David saw the solution.

The same holds true for us and our marriage. We find what we're looking for, we become what we think about, and we get what we expect. We truly do gravitate toward what we contemplate, and it affects every area of life.

THE QUESTION
Do you live problem focused or purpose focused?

The last thing Greg wanted to do was spend Saturday morning in the doctor's office. It had been a long week. The last thing Joshua wanted was a sore throat. Reluctantly, they decided to skip breakfast and quickly jumped in the car to beat the rush to the walk-in clinic. Traffic seemed heavier than normal; then again, Greg wasn't usually out of the house by 8:00 a.m. on Saturday. "I'm starving," Josh said, with a raspy voice. "Let's get Subway."

"We need to hurry and get to the doctor before it gets too busy. We'll grab something when we're done," Greg said hurriedly.

A couple miles down the road, Josh said, "Dad, I never noticed how many Subways there are. They're everywhere—I've counted seven!"

Greg laughed. "Yes, isn't that funny, buddy?" he said. "We find what we're looking for, don't we?"

How about you—have you ever noticed that? You're a little hungry and every commercial on the television advertises restaurants, tempting you with luscious scenes of decadence. You go car shopping and buy a blue Honda and, like magic, suddenly blue Hondas appear everywhere. You find a new blemish or wrinkle on your face, and now every time you get in front of a mirror, it's all you can see.

Here is the question: Do you live problem focused or purpose focused? Getting what we focus on in marriage is fine and well, unless the subject of our marital thoughts centers on our problems. His dirty socks lying beside the laundry hamper, her stories consisting of too many details, his constant interruptions interjected amidst her ideas, the way she talks, the way he chews, the way he or she never does this or that. Or sometimes couples become consumed by weightier issues, like Kaden and Mia did.

A Shift in Thinking

Kaden fidgeted slightly, rubbing his hands against his freshly pressed jeans, his silence at first misinterpreted as disinterest. Mia, on the other hand, couldn't wait to talk about the problems in their marriage. For an hour and a half, she reflected on the various turning points of their marriage, how they met, what was lacking in their relationship, and the ongoing confusion surrounding it. After two and a half decades of marriage, they had a lot to talk about—frustrations, disappointments, obstacles needing hurdled, but none more impeding than their separation for the last two years.

Finally, Kaden spoke up. He fixed his eyes on ours, fearful of Mia's response. "I want to make things work but I need Mia to forgive me." Immediately, Mia's countenance changed. She shifted in her chair and crossed her arms. Kaden continued, rather timidly: "I know I've really messed up and that it's hard for Mia to trust me. But I'm at a loss and feel powerless to fix it."

Mia rolled her eyes and shook her head. "Well, that's the first time you've ever said that," she blurted out, then sat rigidly awaiting another occasion to point the blame. Kaden's long battle with porn addiction and lack of interest in Mia, sexually, provided fertile soil for roots of anger and bitterness to plant firmly in Mia's soul. Instinctively, she kept her guard up.

After hours of asking questions to reveal the occurrences that led them to where they were, it was time to move forward on common ground. "Do you want to get better?" Greg asked. "Do you want this marriage to work, or do you want to keep on doing what you've been doing and let your relationship fail?"

Stunned, Mia sat forward and bravely said that she wanted it to work. Kaden concurred and over the next two days we helped them discover and define their unified purpose. Their focus evolved from being problem focused to purpose focused as they embraced this simple truth: Each of them held a distinct God-given purpose, and so did their marriage. The result was that Kaden moved back into their home.

Isn't it astonishing what a shift in thinking promotes when we resist the temptation to focus our attention on what is lacking, what needs improving, and what needs to be fixed? It is truly amazing when we change the subject of our thinking from the Goliaths of the world, the obstacles, and the problems, to focus on the solution. As couples, we experience a greater fulfillment and intimacy when we keep the purpose of our marriage at its center.

Don't be confused. We aren't saying problems, adversity, and conflict don't exist; unfortunately, they're a part of every relationship. However, the solution, the triumph, and the victory for our marriage hinges on our ability to shift our focus from our personal Goliaths to the magnitude of God's power and purpose for our relationship. When couples begin to shift their attention from the problem and focus on living God's purpose, life happens.

A Deeper Look at Scripture

In his book *Think on These Things,* John C. Maxwell writes, "How you think determines who you are. That's why Scripture directs us to be careful about where we focus our attention."[8] Time and time again throughout Scripture, God teaches this principle and encourages us not to be conformed to the world, but to be transformed by the renewing of our mind,[9] and to put off the old man with all its deceitful ways and be renewed in the spirit of our mind.[10]

In Philippians, Paul writes, "Whatever is true, whatever is noble, whatever is right, whatever is pure, whatever is lovely, whatever is admirable — if anything is excellent or praiseworthy — think about such things."[11] One of the greatest ways we participate with God is by yielding our thoughts to Him. Contrary to popular belief, we are not powerless to our thoughts.

AN INTROSPECTIVE CHALLENGE

In what ways do we easily focus on God's power, provision, and purpose? In what areas do we need to redirect our attention?

The Bible promises that "God did not give us a spirit of timidity, but a spirit of power, of love and of self-discipline."[12] Scripture assures us that as couples we can demolish arguments and destroy every lie opposing who God says we are. How do we do this? Only by capturing our thoughts and making them obedient to Christ.[13] When Goliath snarls and says your marriage isn't strong enough, you can smile and reply that God is. When Goliath says you'll never accomplish that together, you simply reply that God says we can. And when Goliath says you don't own enough resources, point to heaven and remember where your help comes from.

God formed you for such a time as this. He designed you distinctly for a purpose and equipped you with everything you need to complete it. His divine power gives you everything you need to fulfill your marriage purpose.[14] Your strengths, weaknesses, and even your lineage all play a part in God's masterful design to shape, prepare, and then position the two of you to fulfill His intended design together. He's inviting you to embrace your collective design by focusing your attention on His intention for your marriage, to exchange your problems for His ultimate purpose.

> A Thought from Stephen R. Covey
> *We see the world, not as it is, but as we are—or, as we are conditioned to see it.*[15]

We gravitate toward what we contemplate, so naturally when we focus on our problems, we reap the subject of our focus—the problem. When we search for opportunities to live out God's design, we look for and find our purpose.

A great philosopher, Michel de Montaigne, once wrote, "The secret of a happy life is to live for a dream that is bigger than you are."[16] Do you dream for something bigger than you are? What consumes you and your spouse's thoughts? Do you live more problem focused or purpose focused? Don't answer for your spouse. Consider your own thoughts.

AN INTENTIONAL APPLICATION

Stop focusing on the problem. Instead, focus on your ideal marriage. Envision what you'd like your marriage to look like, align that vision with God's Word, and then live it out.

Since our thoughts hold power and where we place our focus largely determines our outcome, it's vital we understand our tendencies. The following exercise was designed to help you determine your natural pattern of thought. Take a moment to evaluate your current trend of thinking by highlighting whichever statement best describes your natural inclination. As with any test, you may try to categorize the different areas of your life and get confused. Don't get caught up with thoughts like, *When I'm in a family situation I'm more like this, but if I'm at work I tend to be more like that.* Rather, highlight your answers with a specific regard to your marriage relationship. Make note of where your thoughts focus most frequently.

Remember, the following tool is meant to help you, not condemn you. It displays two contrasting checklists to discern if you live more problem focused or purpose focused in your thoughts.

PROBLEM FOCUSED	PURPOSE FOCUSED
i see my spouse's shortcomings, flaws, and weaknesses.	i see differences in me and my spouse that complement and balance one another.
my spouse's idiosyncrasies constantly annoy me.	i extend grace because i need grace. i choose to believe the best about my spouse, celebrating his or her design.
i tend to complain about the present and the past.	i intentionally practice praise, looking with positive expectancy toward the future. i'm not bound by unforgiveness.
i feel hindered.	i focus on God's promises because they offer me strength and hope.
i lack clarity and am confused by current circumstances.	i am seeking clear direction and certainty of where i want to go.
i tend to see glitches, hitches, and difficulties.	i practice an attitude of gratitude and praise.
i contemplate and point out ways my spouse should change.	i ask God to help my spouse live fully into his design for his or her life. i choose to focus on how i can improve, knowing i can only change myself.
i feel trapped.	i see options and seek God to make positive changes in my life.
i justify my actions by pointing to my spouse's.	i refuse to keep a scoreboard and take accountability to change and grow.
i regret marrying my spouse.	God designed a purpose for my marriage and uses it to make me stronger.
our past and present circumstances hinder us from serving others.	The entirety of our life serves a purpose.
We spend the majority of our time trying to fix one another.	We practice healthy self-examination and genuinely seek to grow together.
i feel burdened to make things happen.	i'm faithful where God positions me.
i often pray, Surely there must be more to life than this.	i most often pray, Father, open the doors You want me to walk through.
i tend to compare and compete, feeling unworthy or inadequate.	i embrace our unique designs and love using our talents for God's glory.

Now tally the number of times you highlighted a purpose-focused statement and compare your number with the sections identified below.

- If you scored 13–15, congrats! You firmly believe God destined you for greatness and aren't intimidated to live it. You master your thoughts. More than likely, people single you out as an optimist. You probably hold a keen idea of God's purpose for your life and love your marriage. Keep up the good work and maintain your humility. You're well on your way to discovering God's exact purpose for your marriage if you haven't already.
- If you scored 10–12, bravo! You generally believe God designed you for a distinct purpose. You tend to focus on what is good over the bad and aren't afraid to practice discipline to ensure you control your thoughts. You enjoy your spouse and share great expectancy toward your future. You truly desire significance, yet at times find yourself lost in the specifics. No worries. Continue to take every thought captive to the cross and, in due time, you will reap great rewards. Keep on keeping on— your distinct marriage purpose awaits you.
- If you scored 7–9, you're a fighter, determined to press forward. You often find yourself frustrated, wanting to be further along and more free in your thoughts—but don't get discouraged. Use your energy to meet with God in prayer. Invite Him to continue to change the things that need to be changed. When you can't change the way you feel, you need to change the way you think. Practice believing the best about your spouse. Speak the power of God's Word over your relationship. Choose to believe that God designed a purpose for your marriage and you

will find it. We are so excited for you to experience greater breakthrough throughout the remainder of this book.

- If you scored 6 or below, then recognize that your natural tendency focuses on the problems that seem to bombard you in your everyday thinking. You try to be positive but feel powerless to the problems surrounding your life. At times you may feel forgotten, defeated, or shortchanged. You may readily recognize obstacles or barriers out of your control that keep you from moving forward in the direction you want to move. Remember, God has not given you a spirit of timidity but the power of a strong mind. Submit your thoughts to Him in prayer. Take time every day to meditate on the truth that God created you and your spouse on purpose and for a purpose. Claim the promises of His Word and never give up. God uses all things for the good of those who love Him.[17] He fights for you and will help you protect what the Enemy tries to steal. You truly are destined for greatness. God designed a purpose for you and your spouse, and we can't wait for Him to reveal it to you.

> A Thought from John C. Maxwell
> *Your life today is a result of your thinking yesterday.*
> *Your life tomorrow will be determined by what you think today.*[18]

Our thoughts become our actions, our actions become our habits, our habits become our character, and our character defines who we are. Who we are determines *how we do everything*. Thus, the power of our focus truly impacts our outcome. True, our Goliaths are big, but our God is bigger, and He's still in the giant-slaying business. His purpose for our marriage already exists and He will equip us, fill us, and empower us to live life to its fullest.[19]

But, like David, we must participate. Aristotle said, "We are what we repeatedly do."[20] So let's repeatedly align our thoughts with God's perspective. How do we do this? By praying daily, meditating on His Word, and then demonstrating our faith by focusing on His purpose for our marriage, not the magnitude of the problem.

Study Guide: Chapter 3

Our thoughts become our actions, and our actions produce results. If we want different results in our life and different results in our marriage, then it begins with a change in our thoughts. As you and your spouse talk together, ask God to show you the ways you need to change your thinking from being problem focused to purpose focused.

Questions to Consider

1. We judge others by their actions and their results, but we judge ourselves by our intentions. As a couple, how can you practice believing the best about one another?

2. Jesus said, "Again, I tell you that if two of you on earth agree about anything you ask for, it will be done for you by my Father in heaven. For where two or three come together in my name, there am I with them."[21] Ask, Do we really believe this passage? And, if so, What keeps us from dreaming together? How can we begin to believe bigger? (For example, does comfort stop you, do you allow the everyday status quo to hold you back, or do setbacks discourage your belief?)

3. Continue asking, *God, what do You want us to believe together?*

4. In what practical ways can you shift your focus from fear and problems to God's power and purpose for your marriage? (For example, we try to recognize and verbally

celebrate each day's successes. We constantly evaluate our *whys*, like, Why are we participating in this activity? or, Why do we serve in this area?)

5. What checkpoints can we establish to recognize old habits so we can remove them and move toward purpose-focused living?

Scriptures to Study

- Proverbs 23:7
- Matthew 18:18–20
- Mark 12:31
- John 10:10
- Romans 12:1
- 2 Corinthians 10:5–6
- Ephesians 4:22–24
- 2 Peter 1:3
- Philippians 4:8
- 2 Timothy 1:7

A Simple Prayer

Father, help us to focus on who You are, not on our giants. Help us to truly see one another's best qualities. Show us how our unique designs and differences further Your purpose. Help us to live purpose focused, not problem focused, and empower us to truly discover Your purpose for our marriage and then live it out in our everyday lives. In Your name we ask, amen.

Chapter 4

HOW DOES GOD CONFIRM HIS PURPOSE?

A Timeless Truth
God reveals His purpose for your marriage through His Word, confirms His plans through your circumstances, and affirms ongoing direction through people.

At some point in our journey to live out God's purpose for our marriage, we'll need to evaluate our beliefs. We are not referring to what others expect us to believe, not even what we've been taught to profess, but in all good conscience (to the very core of our soul) we consider who we really believe God to be and what He has called us to do.

This is important because no couple ever reaches their destiny in a single leap. Instead, we fulfill our marriage purpose by putting one foot in front of the other, moving in the direction of where God leads us one day at a time, and by constantly evaluating, What has God called us to? What promise has He whispered to us? And where is He leading us now? Pretty simple, huh?

Yet how often do we meander through life, never asking those questions? Or, when we do take the time to ask them, we wonder if we possess the ability to discern God's purpose. Thankfully, God reinforces His directions clearly, confidently, and concisely. In this chapter, we'll share three key ways God confirms His purpose for our marriage.

If you're willing to continue the journey to discover the riches of your marriage purpose but feel hesitant because you don't know what to do next or fearful of where you may end up, take courage as we step back in time to take a peek at two heroes of the faith who probably shared similar feelings.

A Discovery from God's Word

> "Leave your country, your people and your father's household and go to the land I will show you. I will make you into a great nation and I will bless you."[1]

Abram's weathered wrinkles confirmed his uncertainties; his graying hair affirmed his physical limitations. By all earthly standards, Abram wasn't exactly a prime candidate to receive the Father of Many Nations Award. Thankfully, however, God didn't need anyone else's opinion. He likes to operate like that. God chooses the unlikely to accomplish the unbelievable, the underdog to undertake the unimaginable, and the improbable to reveal the incredible. Abram's story reminds us that God uses the weak, the weary, and the imperfect to accomplish the impossible, thus providing hope for each of us.

At seventy-five years old, Abram heard God's shocking promise—a promise of blessing, a promise of significance, a promise he could barely believe but did. Abram's hazel eyes glistened and sparkled slightly as he recalled God's promises spoken only a few weeks earlier: "Leave your country, your people and your father's household and go to the land I will show you. I will make you into a great nation and I will bless you."[2]

HOW DOES GOD CONFIRM HIS PURPOSE?

Abram laughed aloud, excited to finally be leaving. "Sarai, Sarai! My love! My beautiful bride and darling mother-to-be—where are you? Ah, there you are." In a single swoop, Abram spun Sarai into his arms and held her body firmly to his: "C'mon, sweet cheeks, it's time to go." Abram swatted Sarai's backside and wiggled his eyebrows.

"Whew. You steal my breath." Abram paused, admiring Sarai's beauty. At sixty-five years old, she still captivated his attention. Abram softly whispered in her ear as he ran his fingers through her long ebony hair. "I am a lucky man," he said.

"Oh, stop!" Sarai giggled softly, dismissing Abram's advances. "Your eyesight's failing you. Now let me go."

Abram studied Sarai's face and noticed a fear he had somehow eluded. "Sarai, everything will be all right," Abram consoled. "God's got this!" Sarai bit the side of her lip, holding back her tears. "We are about to take an adventure of a lifetime," Abram repeated.

Sarai looked at her husband intently. *If this is what it takes to make him happy, I guess I'm in.* Her body relaxed into Abram's arms. *Maybe Abram really did hear from God. Maybe I really will have a baby.* Lost in the moment, Sarah smiled with growing expectation.

"Attagirl!" Abram released Sarai's waist, took a little side step, clicked his heels together, and sashayed toward the door. Sarai loved Abram's confidence. He always seemed so unintimidated by the unknown. He never worried about how his children would come to be or in what time frame they would be born. He never concerned himself with her barrenness—he simply believed God and made arrangements to leave.

Servants? Check.

Sheep? Check.

Cattle...donkeys? Check and check.

Oh, there is so much to do. If only I had a son to help with all the details, Abram thought to himself. *Ha! A son! I'm going to be a father.* Once again, the promise of God distracted him from any fears or potential dangers.

I wonder what we should name him? Maybe Haran, after my brother who died. Maybe Joshua? Michael? Or we could call him Aaron. A small grin formed and then stretched from one ear to the other: *Maybe I'll use all of the names. After all, a mighty nation requires a lot of sons!* Abram's heart skipped a beat. He hadn't felt this young in years.

Isn't it mind-boggling how ecstatic life becomes when God first speaks? How the possibility of what will be overshadows what has been? How momentary realities and limitations cower in the presence of God's promise?

Abram felt invincible. No mountain too high, and no valley too low. No fears and no worries, just an abiding trust in the God who had given him a promise. Sarai's twenty-five years of barrenness were not even on his radar. The misery of his decision to birth Ishmael was unforeseen. Instead, Abram remained blissfully expectant. He felt like many do on their wedding day—full of excitement and expectation, as if he could walk on air. Eventually, Abram realized his journey would be rougher than first expected.

Unfortunately, like Abram and Sarai, we often encounter a rockier terrain than we first anticipated. God's purpose for our marriage sinks beneath mounting bills, increased workloads, and never-ending to-do lists. Our responsibilities seem endless as our tasks overshadow the hours it takes to complete them. Then there are the kids and all the intentionality their needs require. Each undone duty compounds our fears and causes questions to surface such as: How do we know what God is saying? How do we know He's leading and we aren't just making something up? How can we really know our God-given marriage purpose? If that's you, then take heart.

> A Thought from Winston Churchill
> *As long as we have faith in our own cause and an unconquerable will to win, victory will not be denied us.*[3]

Like Abram and Sarai, you might not know all the steps of where God is taking you, but know this: God designed your marriage with a well-defined purpose, and He will faithfully reveal His purpose for your marriage through His Word, confirm His plan through your circumstances, and use people to affirm ongoing direction.

A Deeper Look at Scripture

In John 10, God promises that His sheep will recognize His voice, they will follow His voice, and will not follow a stranger's voice. He assures us He knows His sheep and His sheep know Him. That's good news. According to this passage, we will sense God's voice and be able to distinguish it from our own.

> A Thought from Rick Warren
> *God is not just the starting point of your life; he is the source of it. To discover your purpose in life you must turn to God's Word, not the world's wisdom.*[4]

The one consistent method God uses to reveal His purpose for our marriage is found throughout Scripture. God will never prompt us to do something contrary to His Word (as revealed in the Bible). The more we familiarize ourselves with God's Word, the more we readily distinguish His direction from any imitation. His Word provides direction, purpose, and the measuring stick to discern whether what we're thinking is His idea, our idea, or something else entirely. Simple and practical, yes; but also trustworthy and true.

THE QUESTION
How can we spend more time—together—enjoying God's Word, and help each other better recognize His voice?

Several years ago, God called us to step away from our lucrative careers. Eventually, trials tested us and we questioned whether or not we'd heard God accurately. Had He really called us out of corporate America? What if we had made up His purpose for our marriage? Had He really called us to write, speak, and coach couples? We tried dismissing our doubts, but as the storm raged on, we found it increasingly difficult to believe.

One evening, at the height of the storm, we desperately cried out, *Father, please quiet our fears. Confirm Your steps. Help!* Later that evening God awakened us to comforting thoughts, promising to make the rough places smooth and to open doors that no one could shut. As the promises filled our mind, we felt prompted to get up and read Isaiah 45. Here's where it really gets awe inspiring. As we read from Isaiah 45, a passage neither of us knew by heart, we read similar words promising that God would open doors for us,[5] that He would go before us and level mountains and break down gates,[6] and that He would make our paths straight and would raise us up again.[7] The entire passage confirmed we were on the right path, despite our trials.

The promises God whispered that evening, though astounding, would not be enough for the barrage of attacks we faced in the weeks and months to come; we daily needed God's direction. God's Word secured His direction, and, as the psalmist wrote, was a light to our path.[8]

A Thought from John Ruskin
The highest reward for a man's toil is not what he gets for it but what he becomes by it.[9]

Every couple desiring to live God's purpose eventually faces battles against the Enemy, who wants to stop them from living God's purpose for their marriage. During those battles, positive mental attitude isn't enough; at least not if your battles are like the ones we have faced. God's Word alone provides the encouragement necessary to live your marriage purpose. His Word reminds us that He strongly supports those who are His,[10] that He leads the steps of the righteous and gives strength to the weary,[11] that He uses *all* things—the things perceived as good and the things perceived as bad—for your good.[12]

God rescued us through His living, breathing Word.[13] During our darkest season, He made sense out of what seemed senseless and nurtured us with a peace surpassing all understanding.[14] That's *who* God is; that's what His Word provides. As you move forward to pinpoint His unquestionable purpose for your marriage, remember that He reveals His purpose for your marriage through His Word and often confirms His plans through your circumstances.

God Often Reveals His Purpose for Your Marriage through Circumstances

Shortly after God directed us out of corporate America, He began prompting us to sell our home, which was *not* something we wanted to do. Nothing in us wanted to move. We loved our home, we loved our church, and we loved our community. Yet we felt compelled to put our house on the market. Like Abram and Sarai, we felt like God called us out but the details of where He called us to weren't quite yet clear. Instead of a full, step-by-step, A–Z guide, God required us to take the first of many steps—we needed to sell our home.

Not being flighty people, we researched the market, planned interviews with realtors, and googled ideas on how to sell our home quickly. We found several interesting articles offering a vast array of ideas on what to do to sell our home. Among the items listed appeared the words *display yellow flowers*. The research suggested that yellow flowers invoked a buying impulse in people who were looking at your home. For some reason, the idea stuck in our minds, along with making our house smell like homemade cookies and decluttering shelving space.

After getting the kids off to school, Julie drove to the local market, determined to purchase a bouquet of yellow flowers for display. As she perused the store, looking for the yellow beauties, she silently prayed, *Father, these are big decisions. We need to know what You want. Please confirm whether or not we're on the right path.*

Apparently, Kentucky didn't yield a lot of yellow flowers in early spring, so she left with a concession of mixed flowers, not knowing what was about to happen once she arrived home.

"I left a package on your front porch," the delivery man said while smiling.

"Oh, thank you." Julie smiled and waved as she walked toward the front of our house.

Wow, my husband's so awesome, Julie thought as she peered inside the beautifully wrapped bouquet of yellow lilies. *I can't believe he took the time to send such a thoughtful gift.* But it didn't take long to realize a greater love than Greg's compelled the purchase. Julie read the attached note:

> You were in my waking thoughts. As I prayed, the line "remember the lilies of the fields" came to mind. I knew I was supposed to send you lilies, specifically yellow.
>
> Love, Amy

God prompted a very dear friend (who was *not* privy to our yellow flower discussion, or our inclination to sell our home, and who was over eleven hundred miles from where we lived) to send us a bouquet of yellow lilies. Why? Because God uses circumstances to confirm our steps. As we said yes to God's purpose and obediently followed His lead, He affirmed our steps by using yellow flowers to inspire us with additional confirmation of His direction.

We could go on and on with the ways God confirmed our steps. In 2008, for example, during the height of the market crash, we sold our home in just five short days. Then, when He began dealing with our hearts to move again, after only living in Texas for five months, God confirmed our steps once again—the owners of the house we rented from suddenly and unexpectedly decided to move back from Europe. Coincidental? No way. God moved on our hearts to consider moving to Florida and within twenty-four hours after asking Him to confirm His promptings, we were asked to vacate our home.

We know many of you may be asking, *Do you really believe God is that personal?* Oh my goodness, yes. Think about it. All throughout Scripture, God demonstrates that He uses all things to confirm His purpose for His people. He offered Mary comfort when John the Baptist leaped within Elizabeth's womb,[15] and He reassured Joseph through dreams.[16] At Gideon's request, He confirmed His purpose by saturating a fleece and surrounding it with dry ground. And then, at a second request, God saturated the dry ground but kept the fleece dry.[17] For Moses, He turned a rod into a snake to reassure him that He was with him.[18] Sometimes we want God to fill in all the sketchy details with a go-do-this and go-do-that kind of list. Instead, God typically calls each one of us to walk our journey in faith, and, as we faithfully follow, He confirms His purpose through His Word and affirms His purpose though our circumstances.

> **AN INTROSPECTIVE CHALLENGE**
> God directs us through His Word, confirms it through our circumstances, and surrounds us with key people to affirm His direction, but it all begins by asking: Lord, what do You desire for our marriage?

God will confirm your marriage purpose, especially when you actively look for His confirmation. Remember that you find what you're looking for. Pay attention to the details surrounding your life. Don't fabricate His voice; rather, recognize and acknowledge it. Expect Him to confirm His purpose for your marriage and to direct your steps. God's Word says it this way: "You will seek me and find me when you seek me with all your heart."[19] God truly will lead you through His Word and confirm your marriage purpose through the circumstances surrounding your life. You simply need to pay attention.

God Confirms His Purpose for Our Marriage through People

Though circumstances and confirmation through people remains subjective, when we line up our life with God's Word, He confirms His will through our experiences and affirms our steps through the people we encounter along our journey. Together, as you follow God's lead, He will faithfully connect you with instrumental people to fulfill His purpose. He's the master of divine connections. David, while out shepherding his father's flock, caught the attention of Saul's servant, a connection that positioned David in the palace.[20] Wise men who were led by a star knelt with gifts before Mary and Joseph.[21] Even Abimelech offered Abraham gifts in exchange for his pardon.[22]

In *The Purpose Driven Life*, Rick Warren writes, "Spiritual gifts and natural abilities are always confirmed by others."[23] As we look back over our lives, we recognize all the people God surrounded our lives with who confirmed our marriage purpose in order to provide pathways to sustainable growth and life transformation. From the moment we married, our pastor positioned us to lead a marriage class. From the day we said I do, God used our transparency to inspire couples to renew their love for one another.

Everywhere we go, we hear things like, "You guys are amazing individually, but together...wow! Now that's the special sauce!" Pastors welcome us into their inner circle and confirm God's purpose for our marriage by sharing their struggles and seeking our advice. In business, it's no different. Presidents and CEOs seek our insights, both professionally and personally. How is God confirming His purpose for your marriage? How is He directing your purpose through your circumstances and connections?

Learning from Others

As we work with couples, it's easy to notice how they complement one another. When we met John and Kayla, we easily recognized their passion to build solid relationships with their kids. They always provided the go-to house for other kids to hang out at. As their kids invited friends over, they led multiple teenagers to express a belief in Christ by demonstrating God's love within their family. They never held a formal role in the pulpit, but you better believe they impacted hundreds of kids. As their own children grew, we helped them funnel their purpose into helping other young couples establish similar values into their family structure.

On your path of discovering God's purpose for your marriage, be sure to look for opportunities to learn from other people. Begin asking questions, like, Who encourages us and who do we like to encourage? Where do we see the most fruit from our life? For what recurring reason do people reach out to us? Seriously examine the evidence—it's right in front of you. Be intentional to notice what others seem to notice about you, remembering that God affirms His plans through people and arranges relationships to empower you in your journey of discovering your marriage purpose.

AN INTENTIONAL APPLICATION
Consider how God is speaking to you through His Word, confirming through your circumstances, and affirming through others.

We've gone to great lengths to reveal three foundations necessary to continue in your journey toward the details of your marriage purpose. So take a moment to consider the intentional application listed above and then discuss your answers further in this chapter's study guide section.

Study Guide: Chapter 4

Questions to Consider

1. James 1:5 says, "If any of you lacks wisdom, he should ask God, who gives generously to all without finding fault, and it will be given to him." How has God confirmed His purpose for your marriage through His Word? (Has a particular Scripture ever caused the two of you to sense His purpose for your marriage? If so, write it down and ask God for further direction. If not, then ask Him to speak to the two of you as you read His Word together.)

2. How has God confirmed His purpose for your marriage through circumstances? Ask one another: Are there doors God wants us to step through that we've been dragging our heels, or others we've tried to kick open that God wants kept closed? How can we use our gifts, practically, right where we are?

3. How has God confirmed His purpose for your marriage through people? Take a few minutes to consider who inspires you and where you add the most value to others. Where is the evidence of the greatest fruit of your life?

Scriptures to Study

- Genesis 12:1–3; 20:14–16
- Exodus 4:3–4
- Numbers 22:27–30
- Judges 6:36–40
- 1 Samuel 16:18

Study Guide: Chapter 4

- Matthew 1:20; 2:12–13, 19, 22; 2:10–11
- Luke 1:41
- 2 Timothy 4:5
- Hebrews 4:12
- James 1:5

A Simple Prayer

God, Your Word promises that You will grant us wisdom and lead our steps. Help us to discern Your perfect plan for our marriage. We want to say yes to You, but sometimes it's hard to discern Your voice. Give us ears to hear and a willingness to listen to how You are leading us through Your Word, confirming Your purpose through our circumstances, and affirming Your purpose for our marriage through others.

Chapter 5

WHY ARE WE SO DIFFERENT?

A Timeless Truth
Devaluing one another's difference leads
to dishonor ... Dishonor instigates dissension ...
And dissension precedes destruction.

One thing's for certain: Marriage affords plenty of opportunity for offense. What once caught our intrigue, if not protected, can easily cause our irritation. It's found in all the "He never talks. She never shuts up. He's so particular. She never pays attention to details. He's a night owl. She gets up before the rooster. He flies by the seat of his pants. She schedules next year's spring cleaning," and thus it goes on and on. There is a myriad of trivial differences that discourage and distract couples from their purpose. Julie: "Is he really making another best friend at the gas pump? Seriously, Greg, we're already running late." Greg: "Julie, give 'em a 20 percent tip, for crying out loud. What's the difference of a dollar or two?"

Be on guard. A house divided against itself will fall.[1] Hold up. Don't breeze by this familiar truth. If we devalue one another, we eventually dishonor one another. If we dishonor one another, then dissension grows between us. When dissension escalates, destruction becomes inevitable. A house divided against itself will not stand—a truth Michal, David's wife, realized all too late.

A Discovery from God's Word

> As the ark of the covenant of the Lord was entering the City of David, Michal daughter of Saul watched from a window. And when she saw King David dancing and celebrating, she despised him in her heart.[2]

Excitement traveled throughout the street. David's laughter rang above the instruments. "Oh, Lord, You promised this day. Be exalted in it."

With unhindered, unreserved abandon, David leaped before the Lord. Perspiration saturated his outer robe. "Whew, it's hot." David turned toward his brother-in-law Jonathan. "Hey, hold my robe for me." David smirked as he stripped to his linen undergarment.

Jonathan laughed out loud. "Oh, if only I could be so free."

David winked, nodding toward the eligible maidens lining the celebration. "C'mon then, brother, I'm sure we could find a few girls who'd gladly hold your robe." David egged on Jonathan to join in the merriment.

"Oh, no," Jonathan said. "I fear the king would disown me should I dance so freely."

David laughed. "Well then, hold fast to my robe and bring it to your sister's home this evening." With that, David danced even more vigorously than he had before. He was exuberant before the Lord, absolutely uninhibited.

Michal's lady-in-waiting called to her mistress. "My lady, come quickly. Look at your husband."

"Where is he?" Michal asked. "I can't wait to see him."

"Just there—see, on the other side of the ark." Michal's attendant pointed.

Instantly, Michal's beaming face soured and turned to a scowl. She looked on in absolute disbelief. *What is he doing in his undergarment? Look at him dancing and thrashing around.* David's jubilation spoiled Michal's exhilaration. Her heightened anticipation of his return was ruined. Michal watched David's every move with growing suspicion. Her spirit raged as every maiden swooned when her husband passed by. Each time David leaped, Michal's heart dropped.

Well, isn't that just glorious, Michal thought as she paced back and forth on their balcony, seething with anger. *Where is his propriety? Where is his dignity? If he thinks I'll just stand by and watch him show himself to every maiden in the land, he has another thing coming.*

The festivities lasted well into the evening, but David eagerly turned his attention toward home, anxious to see his bride. "Michal! I'm home," he shouted. "You should have seen the..." Michal met David in the corridor. Her dagger-like glare interrupted his celebration.

She snarled with disgust. "How the king of Israel has distinguished himself today, disrobing in the sight of the slave girls of his servants as any vulgar fellow would!"[3]

Can you imagine David's shock? Instead of admiration, Michal admonished David. Instead of celebrating his victory, she criticized and condemned him. Instead of joining in his jubilation, Michal judged. At the height of one of David's greatest pinnacles of success, Michal imposed formalities and felt compelled to correct him. Maybe, in Michal's defense, she needed to protect David. Maybe she thought, *A king doesn't act like that. A king acts with decorum. A king acts with decency. David has obviously forgotten himself. My father will never honor a man who acts so undignified.* Regardless of motive, Michal's actions communicated contempt and provoked David's anger.

You have got to be kidding me, David thought. *It's been over a year since we've embraced and you're going to greet me with disdain? How dare you disrespect me or disapprove of my dancing before the Lord.* Enraged, David reacted, saying, "It was before the Lord, who chose me rather than your father or anyone from his house when he appointed me ruler over the Lord's people Israel—I will celebrate before the Lord. I will become even more undignified than this, and I will be humiliated in my own eyes. But by these slave girls you spoke of, I will be held in honor."[4] With that, David dismissed Michal from his presence. And the Bible gives us the sober statement: "And Michal daughter of Saul had no children to the day of her death."[5]

Intense, eh? What should have been a moment of unification ended in separation. What could have been a moment of celebrating life resulted in a bereavement of barrenness. How about you? Have you ever encountered moments when your escalated emotions, even if well intended, clashed with your spouse's and caused dissension; moments when, instead of seeking to understand them, you tried to fix them and ended up undermining them?

It's easy to look at Michal and David's story and distinguish ways they could have prevented their fallout. David could have looked past Michal's offenses and recognized her insecurities. He could have comforted her and sought to understand how he might have felt had she innocently paraded in her underwear up and down the street lined with eligible warriors. Michal could have pushed aside her insecurities and concerns of propriety and simply celebrated David's enthusiasm.

But what about our differences with our spouse—how can we welcome one another's perspectives and varying personalities? God, in His wisdom, created us differently—but why? Why would God design us so distinctly? What's the greater purpose of our diversity?

WHY ARE WE SO DIFFERENT?

> A Thought from Andrew Carnegie
> *It marks a big step in your development when you come to realize that other people can help you do a better job than you can do alone.*[6]

THE QUESTION
Why are we so different?

In his book *Positive Personality Profiles,* Dr. Robert A. Rohm writes, "If I understand you and you understand me, doesn't it make sense that we can have a better relationship?"[7] Dr. Rohm's study of the four personality styles wasn't designed to determine the best personality or to classify a personality as either right or wrong; instead, his study promotes understanding between personality types. One of the greatest opportunities presented in marriage is appreciating our spouse's differences—not just tolerating them, but actually celebrating them.

No doubt you've read the proverb, "As iron sharpens iron, so one person sharpens another."[8] As believers, we tend to celebrate this great saying with a high five or a chest-bump sort of merriment. We envision lifting each other and encouraging one another, as we well should. But in our enthusiasm we sometimes overlook the reality of the process. How do you suppose one piece of iron sharpens another? Is it their likenesses or their differences that deliver the provision?

Think about it for a moment. For one piece of iron to sharpen another piece of iron, friction is imperative. Sharpening occurs as one smooth, sharp edge of iron rubs against a separate rough edge of iron. As the two edges connect, the rough edge grinds away to reveal a smooth, sharp edge. Thus, it is the differences, not the similarities, that supply the friction necessary to produce the sharpening. Hmm, does that sound like your marriage?

In *The Marriage Makeover,* Phillip Wagner writes, "We make a great leap in maturity when we realize we have differences because God made us that way—not because one of us is flawed and the other is not."[9] In a marriage relationship, God desires us to funnel our focus on celebrating and leveraging one another's differences. He intended our diversities. When we embrace them as an opportunity for growth, we experience remarkable results and accomplish more together than we would separately. Our differences expose our blind spots and magnify our strengths to multiply our impact.

> A Thought from Malcom Forbes
> *Diversity: the art of thinking independently together.*[10]

In their book *Strengths Based Leadership,* Tom Rath and Barry Conchie share that as they worked with executive leadership teams and conducted interviews to discover what made those teams great, they "began to see that while each member had his or her own unique strengths, the most cohesive and successful teams possessed broader groupings of strengths."[11] We sure wish we had read their insights a couple decades ago. It would have spared us a lot of pain if we'd looked at our differences as strengths instead of weaknesses.

Thankfully, we've learned to embrace Malcom Forbes' definition of diversity, which is "the art of thinking independently together," and no longer resist our differences. As a matter of fact, we now welcome our differences, appreciate them, and even admire them. By God's grace, we've come a long way. Today, we embrace and leverage our diversity in order to accomplish God's higher purpose for our marriage. Here's a quick peek at how our differences sharpen us and play out in our marriage.

Gaining an Appreciation for One Another

We both love to lead in business and faith settings. Yet our leadership styles vary greatly. One isn't better than the other, yet each style may be better for an individual situation. Greg carries a commanding yet inspiring presence. He possesses a keen ability to expose areas that need to be improved and exhorts individuals toward excellence. He empowers them to run through what once felt like brick walls and hurdle over what once felt impossible. He leaves no room for excuses. On the other hand, Julie influences through love and encouragement. She inspires people to grow by reminding them of who God created them to be and to hold fast to the promises He's given them. People are drawn to her like Mother Teresa, rallying around her because they sense her sincerity and purity of heart. They get on board and support her without her even asking.

In the past, we looked at one another's differences and felt compelled to change them. We used to drive each other crazy as we observed the other in action. Julie felt downright uncomfortable when Greg directly addressed the proverbial elephant in the room. Julie: "Why do you *always* need to be the one to bring up such confrontational subjects?" Greg: "Everyone else was thinking it. I just addressed it so we could deal with it and move past it." In yet another scenario, Greg scratched his head, thinking, *How'd she get them to do that? Some of her thoughts didn't even connect. She needs to streamline her presentations and be more straightforward with her team.* We nearly drove one another crazy trying to change one another as Greg addressed elephants in the room and Julie wandered down bunny trails.

Over the years, as we gained appreciation for one another, we entered a different phase and tried to mimic one another's style. That didn't work at all. As a matter of fact, it was sort of like trying on one another's underwear (though you'll be happy to know we've never actually tried that). As you can imagine, it just wouldn't work.

And *that* is exactly why we consciously celebrate our differences. We realize God uniquely uses us and gifted us individually in such a way that our differences enhance His purpose for our marriage.

> **A Thought from Les and Leslie Parrott**
> *Making a cross-gender relationship work does not depend solely on recognizing our differences. It's a matter of appreciating those differences....*[12]

Believing the best about one another and celebrating our differences impacts every part of our marital relationship. Instead of comparing or competing for whose way is better, we discern how our differences actually complement one another. For example, we both love people and value building relationships. Greg draws firm lines to navigate difficult yet necessary conversations, while Julie leans on that strength, and follows with gentle words of encouragement to communicate value. We both care deeply about building people up and assisting them to move forward into God's design. As we intentionally celebrate our differences, we maximize God's perfect design and learn to operate in the rhythm He intended for our marriage. Instead of trying to change one another, we actually value one another and appreciate our differences, knowing that two are better than one.

How about you? How do your differences add dimension to your marriage? How do they harmonize to maximize your efforts?

THE QUESTION
How do your differences advance your marriage purpose?

An old Chinese proverb says it this way: "A family in harmony will prosper in everything." Doesn't that sound like a worthy pursuit? It is one certainly more useful than criticizing or trying to change one another. Check out some principles uncovered from

God's Word and run with your spouse in such a way that you add value to one another, embracing and extending one another's differences.

A Deeper Look at Scripture

In marriage, we may not always see eye to eye, we may not agree on everything, and sometimes our differences arise in our beliefs. The early church was no different. It's funny to read some of the subject matter that caused division. In Romans, for example, Paul addresses God's people, encouraging them to stop quarreling over debatable matters. In essence, the early believers faced a quandary. Some ate meat while others didn't. Truthfully, there was a little more going on than just preferential taste. In that day, pagans offered meat as a sacrifice to other gods and then sold it in the marketplace. For some early believers, that knowledge convicted them to abstain from consuming all meats, while for others they felt unbound by others' rituals and ate with certitude of their freedom. Can you see the point of contention? Can you imagine the heated debates surrounding their fellowship over food?

To this divided group, Paul writes, "Accept him whose faith is weak, without passing judgment on disputable matters.... The man who eats everything must not look down on him who does not, and the man who does not eat everything must not condemn the man who does, for God has accepted him."[13]

Obviously, the key to this passage lays in Paul's verbiage of *disputable matters*. In matters of opinion, let's concede and simply agree to disagree, thus building on principles moving us toward God's purpose as outlined in previous chapters. Welcoming our differences and valuing one another's gifts empowers us to follow after God's clues to fulfill the Great Commission, to worship, serve, and bring God pleasure, and to demonstrate unconditional love to all of those around us.

> A Thought from Tom Paterson
> *Your potential for excellence lies within your uniqueness.*[14]

Paul expounds on the importance of embracing our unique design in 1 Corinthians 12 when he writes, "The body is a unit, though it is made up of many parts; and though all its parts are many, they form one body. So it is with Christ. For we were all baptized by one Spirit into one body—whether Jews or Greeks, slave or free—and we were all given the one Spirit to drink. Now the body is not made up of one part but of many."[15]

He then goes on to address the quandary we often struggle with today—what's our part in God's kingdom? What role do we play? How do my talents compare with my spouse's? What's Paul's solution to all of this? He goes on to write:

> If the foot should say, "Because I am not a hand, I do not belong to the body," it would not for that reason cease to be part of the body. And if the ear should say, "Because I am not an eye, I do not belong to the body," it would not for that reason cease to be part of the body. If the whole body were an eye, where would the sense of hearing be? If the whole body were an ear, where would the sense of smell be? But in fact God has arranged the parts in the body, every one of them, just as he wanted them to be.[16]

Are you getting it? God designed us distinctly just as He wanted us to be. Don't misunderstand us here. Obviously, we need to continue to improve and grow, but we need to improve ourselves, not our spouse.

WHY ARE WE SO DIFFERENT?

AN INTROSPECTIVE CHALLENGE
Have I made my spouse my opponent or my partner?

Learning to Appreciate

When we first married, Julie's eye for detail in financial matters seemed strange to Greg. She often questioned receipts or recounted the change through a drive-through window to ensure accuracy. At first, it just seemed a little quirky—then it turned to an annoyance. Eventually, Greg became irritated at Julie poring over receipts. To him it communicated a lack of trust and caused him embarrassment. Julie, on the other hand, just wanted things to be fair. She returned a nickel even if it bowed in her favor. To her, it wasn't a matter of trust, but it was a matter of making things right. Believe it or not, we actually experienced heated arguments over this *disputable matter*. Eventually we realized neither of us was wrong or right; rather, we were merely different—this disputable matter was a matter of our design.

Greg wanted to communicate value and trust, while Julie displayed value by ensuring accuracy. The final breakthrough happened while buying an enormous amount of furniture for our new office. We spent days with the salesperson. We gained so much rapport he would have joined us for Thanksgiving dinner if we'd invited him. Then came the moment for the bill. Throughout the entire day, Julie inadvertently tallied the total purchase in her mind. The bill didn't reflect that total.

"Hmm, that's not right." Julie smiled and pointed at the total.

Greg walked away, embarrassed and enraged. *Unbelievable. I cannot believe you're doing this again.*

"It should be," the sales rep, John, replied. "Let's take a look."

Julie glanced over her right shoulder, seeing Greg's frustration, and thought, *Oh, boy. I did it again.* She then said, "You know what, John? Never mind. It's okay—really," trying to undo what she'd done.

"No. No. No. Let's make sure the total is right," John insisted.

Five minutes later, after composing himself, Greg returned to a jovial exchange. "Your wife just saved you fifteen hundred dollars," John said. "We accidently double-charged you for one of your office desks."

The result is that today Greg happily hands final receipts or contracts for Julie's last-minute glance and Julie relaxes a little more about the nickel she got stiffed at the drive-through window. Together two are better than one.

How about your marriage? Are you opponents or partners? Do you compete or celebrate your unique designs?

AN INTENTIONAL APPLICATION

Consider some ways your differences complement one another.

Before you move on to the next chapter and begin building on common ground, take a moment to reflect on what was written about here. The following study guide lists insightful questions to answer together and Scriptures to reference for further insight.

Study Guide: Chapter 5

Questions to Consider

1. How can you better celebrate one another? Tell your spouse what you appreciate about him or her.

2. Discuss your differences and how they strengthen and complement one another. Share your thoughts with each other.

3. What are some ways you can intentionally defer to one another's strengths?

Scriptures to Study

- Mark 3:24–25
- 2 Samuel 6:20–23
- 1 Corinthians 12:12–26
- Romans 14:1–4

A Simple Prayer

Father, help us to celebrate one another's design instead of competing and thinking my way is the right way. Cause us to recognize how our differences complement one another to accomplish Your purpose for our marriage. We want to live in such a way that from the very depths of our soul we can honestly say, "Thank You for making us so different."

Chapter 6

WHAT'S OUR COMMON GROUND?

A Timeless Truth
Couples who build on common ground
are not easily divided.

On June 16, 1858, Abraham Lincoln delivered an address to his Republican colleagues in the Hall of Representatives: "Mr. President and Gentlemen of the Convention. If we could first know where we are, and whither we are tending, we could then better judge what to do, and how to do it."[1] Later, in that same speech, Abraham Lincoln alluded to Jesus' words, "A house divided against itself cannot stand."[2] Likewise, in marriage, when we identify *where* we are and *where* we are going, we will better judge *what* to do and *how* to do it.

When a couple determines to build on common ground and moves toward a common purpose, their house stands firm and will not be divided. And we can't think of a better biblical couple to illustrate God's design for marriage than Priscilla and Aquila.

A Discovery from God's Word

Greet Priscilla and Aquila, my fellow workers in
Christ Jesus. They risked their lives for me. Not only

I but all the churches of the Gentiles are grateful to them.[3]

Aquila stood to rub his lower back. "Okay, princess. Time to go."
"Already—wow. Okay, just give me one minute." Priscilla wove the final strand of goat's hair tightly through their largest loom and rushed to set it aside. "Who's speaking tonight?"
"A man named Apollo," Aquila responded. "I hear he's quite good."
Priscilla let out a long, exhausted sigh. "I miss him, Aquila. I miss Paul's stories. I miss his insights."
"I miss the extra help," Aquila interjected, attempting to lighten the mood, but Priscilla didn't laugh. "Ah, come here, my love," he said. Aquila put his arm around Priscilla, who softly rested her head on his shoulder. Paul had been a great traveling companion to both of them. "I miss him too. But I heard good news—Paul arrived safely in Antioch. Let's forward some money to help with his expenses."
"That's a great idea," Priscilla said. She then smiled as she ran her fingers across Aquila's perfectly placed laugh lines. "I'll include a few of his favorites too."
For a moment, they lingered together quietly until Priscilla broke their silence. "Oh. I want to drop off a vessel of oil to Mary on our way. I can't imagine being a widow. What my life would look like if I ever lost you…"
"I am pretty amazing," Aquila said whimsically, causing them both to erupt in laughter. Then, as they did everything in life, Priscilla and Aquila ventured together toward the synagogue, hand in hand.
Priscilla quickly grabbed the vessel of oil sitting outside their tent. "Will we have a minute to drop this off?"
"Of course," Aquila said, already planning extra minutes for Priscilla's last-minute missions.

Mary's face lit up, excited to have visitors. "I was just thinking about you," she said.

"Hello, Mary." Priscilla extended Mary the oil and then a warm embrace.

"Oh, thank you. I just used the last bit of mine. How thoughtful of you both!" Mary smiled.

"Any chance you'd like to accompany us to tonight's meeting?" Aquila asked.

"Are you sure I won't be in the way?" Mary asked sheepishly, hoping they really meant their invitation.

"Of course you won't be in the way—we always enjoy your company," Priscilla assured her. She then softly whispered, "Besides, it's always nice to have another female's perspective within the group."

The widow smiled. "Okay. Give me a minute to gather my shawl."

Aquila chuckled, thinking to himself, *Why must women always ask for another minute?*

Priscilla glanced at Aquila from the corner of her eye and smirked as if to say, *I know what you're thinking—we ask for a minute because we know you won't give us longer. Besides, I know that you know me, which is why we left thirty minutes before we needed to.* They both snickered at their keen ability to read one another's thoughts without speaking a word. They couldn't believe they'd already been married forty-seven years.

Since the day they met, they'd been inseparable. They partnered together in business, ministry, and life. Fleeing Rome under Claudius's order only unified and amplified their connection. They pulled together in everything—they learned a new trade and felt compelled to use their talents to lead others to faith. As their business flourished, they used their resources to assist missionaries and others in need. On more than one occasion they furnished shelter and risked their lives for the furtherance of the gospel.

Aquila offered Priscilla a quick wink and whispered, "I love everything about you."

Priscilla flirted back and giggled softly. "I *am* pretty amazing." Once again, both erupted in laughter.

When a couple determines to build on common ground and move toward a common purpose, their house stands firm and will not be divided.

Though Scripture only exposes small glimpses from Priscilla and Aquila's life, one thing's for certain: they mastered the art of building on common ground. Four books of the New Testament show glimpses into their story and highlight ways they embraced God's big idea for their marriage. They did everything together and shared everything in common. They taught and instructed together,[4] they led a church together,[5] and they traveled sharing the gospel together.[6] They impacted others together so greatly that they gained respect and favor from everyone they met.[7] Like the New Testament church, Priscilla and Aquila united together, spiritually, financially, and emotionally.

As Christian couples, we aren't left to play the proverbial pin the tail on the donkey in a pursuit to fulfill our purpose. God grants insights on how to build on common ground in Scripture.

A Deeper Look at Scripture

Drs. Les and Leslie Parrott identify seven qualities of happily married couples. One shared value is "a common spiritual foundation and goal."[8] Building on common ground begins by connecting and growing together spiritually. Our spiritual oneness impacts every other area of life.

God's Word reveals this truth in Acts 2 as the early church intentionally "devoted themselves to the apostles' teaching and the fellowship, to the breaking of bread and the prayers."[9] Do you want to grow together, spiritually, with your spouse? Then devote yourselves to listening to the teaching of God's Word. Join a small marriage group or a couples' Bible study. Take time to worship and pray together, even daily. Make time to connect with God together. The overflow of your spiritual connection will impact other aspects of your relationship just as it did for the early church. Something about their spiritual commitment overflowed into their financial commitment to one another. Acts 2 records that all who believed "were together and had everything in common."[10]

Are we really going to talk about money at this point? you may be thinking. *Now it feels like it is getting really personal.* Seriously though, the topic of finances often causes a rift between couples. Want to know the secret to financial oneness? It begins with spiritually recognizing that everything is a gift from God. We can't even take our next breath unless He permits it. Acknowledging that everything comes from God and belongs to God is the beginning of wisdom—it alleviates the pressure of ownership and positions us as stewards over God's property. Maintaining a heart of stewardship evens the playing field, allowing couples to simply ask: *God, what do You want to do with Your provisions?*

Acts 2 goes on to reveal a strong emotional bond emerging within this growing group of believers. Amidst their busy schedules, believers connected together and committed to fellowship in one another's homes. Don't miss that last sentence. Scripture highlights that as these early believer's praised God and fellowshipped together as families, they enjoyed "the favor of all the people. And the Lord added to their number daily those who were being saved."[11]

Do you want blessing? Significance? Connection? The early church understood that building on common ground—spiritually, financially, and emotionally—perpetuated all three of these. The result? Pentecost and revival. This was a confirmation of God's big idea, that two are indeed better than one.

THE QUESTION
How can you and your spouse build on common ground and reap the benefits of enjoying favor with all people to expand your influence?

Business author Patrick Lencioni, who is the founder and president of the Table Group,[12] shared during the Second Annual Live2Lead Simulcast that "most organizations never synthesize their core values." He went on to explain, "Core values are who we are."

Just as an organization needs to establish who they are in order to succeed, we as couples need to define our core values in order to thrive. Our value system impacts our actions and influences every decision we make. Simply put, who we are determines how we do everything. The couples who readily recognize their core values and establish clear parameters to operate within live with greater vision and experience greater fulfillment.

AN INTROSPECTIVE CHALLENGE
Take a moment to consider,
What values do we share in common?

Obviously, no couple intentionally objects to building on common ground. Many times, it's not a matter of want-to but how-to. What common values do you share? Where do you start? And how do you identify common values?

One of the truths we share during the Married for a Purpose Marriage Reboot Retreat is the importance of identifying and defining core values. Knowing what our core values are allows us to live more true to who we are.

In essence, core values define the principles, beliefs, and standards by which we live. As a couple, understanding one another's values provides additional support to discovering and defining God's purpose for your marriage, as well as growing a deeper appreciation for one another. By understanding your core values and defining them, you declare, *This is who we are! This is how we operate! This is how others recognize us!*

If these values are not upheld or honored by yourself or others, then you will not be able to sustain peace or happiness. Thus, this next exercise is crucial to establishing common ground in your marriage. To get you started, we've provided some core values that others have shared with us over the last almost twenty years of working with couples.

Examples of Core Values

Abundance	determined	faithfulness	love	Significance
Adaptable	discipline	family	legacy	Strong Work ethic
Authenticity	empowerment	friendship	loyalty	
Balance		freedom	People	Self-development
Creativity	encouragement	Grace	Purposeful	Strategic
Companionship	education	honesty	Quality Time	Teachable
Connection	excellence	honor	reliable	Trust
Considerate	fairness	integrity	respect	value
Consistent	faith	impact	results	variety
		Justice	Security	

Obviously, this is not an exhaustive list but it should help you as you begin creating yours. Independently, take a moment to identify your individual core values by answering the following questions.

Using single words, write down your answers.
1. What values make you feel fulfilled or, if missing, make you feel confined or unfulfilled?
2. What values cause you to feel angst if they're taken away or lacking in your life?
3. What helps you feel successful or at peace?
4. In your relationship, what characteristics do you deem most important?

Once you've created your individual list, narrow your answers to your top three to five must-have values. Once you've streamlined your list, share your values with your spouse and communicate why each is so vital to you. As you talk together, you may discover that your spouse listed essential values that you overlooked—add them to your list. After you've both read through your lists, circle any values you share in common and then construct a new list.

You may have a long list at this point in the exercise. Now it's time to identify your core values as a couple by prioritizing your list to your top three to five shared values. Identify your three to five core values by highlighting the ones you both deem extremely important. Congratulations! You've just established one of the major building blocks to fulfilling God's purpose for your lives as a couple. You've identified your shared core values. Consider displaying your list in a place you'll see often.

Leveraging Common Ground

Over the years we've learned the importance of intentionally looking for, finding, celebrating, and leveraging our common ground. We identify shared values, interests, and passions to move us toward our common purpose. In fact, we find the most successful businesses, governments, organizations, and of course marriages build on common values to remain unified in purpose. It starts by identifying core values and then intentionally focusing on building upon them. Over time, building on our core values becomes a habit of thinking. It's just the way you operate—thoughts once problem focused morph to become purpose focused.

> A Thought from Napoleon Hill
> *[Both] success and failure are largely the results of habit!*[15]

Here's how our core values impact our everyday life. At the Gorman household, we are committed to eating dinner together, as a family, around our kitchen table, a minimum of four times a week.

So, what's dinner got to do with a core value? The dinner table represents a new segment of our day. It's the beginning of family time. We intentionally connect by playing a game or asking one another questions. One game we like to play is called High-Low. Have you ever played it? It's simple. One member of the family calls out "high-low" to another member, who then shares a high of their day and a low of their day. As the rules go, you can share two highs if you want but you can never share two lows. Once the person in the proverbial hot seat finishes telling their high and low for the day, they call on a different member to do the same, until everyone has a chance to share. High-low presents a fun, lighthearted way to keep us connected and in touch with one another's lives. As you can imagine, we've shared some great table talk about the real issues, lessons, and successes in life.

As a couple, we also prioritize time together by going out on a date every week. We intentionally look for opportunities to discover one another, like we did when we first began dating. During our date night, we put away our cell phones, we purposely talk about our dreams, and we look for opportunities to touch base on how each other is doing. In short, we intentionally connect.

Looking deeper, you might ask: Why? Why do you hold so fast to these types of commitments? Why is dinner around the table so crucial? Why is date night at the top of your priorities? The answer resides in the core values we share. We both value family and authenticity. Since we both share these same values, family mealtime isn't a have-to, but it's a get-to of life. Date nights aren't a chore—they're a necessity. If we go too long without either, we feel like something's missing.

> A Thought from Tom Paterson
> *People who are moving within their gifts and developing their gifts rarely feel as if they are working. The effort seems more like recreation or play.*[16]

In his book *Education through Recreation*, philosopher L. P. Jacks writes,

> A master in the art of living draws no sharp distinction between his work and his play; his labor and his leisure; his mind and his body; his education and his recreation. He hardly knows which is which. He simply pursues his vision of excellence through whatever he is doing, and leaves others to determine whether he is working or playing.[17]

What do you love to do? What needs to be in place for you to enjoy living life to its fullest? Behind your answers you'll discover your core values, your driving forces, and hints pointing you toward the mottos of your life, which, in turn, point you toward God's design for your marriage.

Our Life Mottos

We've enjoyed deciphering our core values and actually created life mottos from them. Our life mottos express the principles we live by. Some instruct, some inspire, and some simply recap the fundamental beliefs we adhere to. Each life motto conveys direction and governs how we live every day of our lives. Each motto stems from our core values of purpose, faith, and family. They inspire us to live for more, to reach for more, to be more. They challenge us to remember who's really in control and whom we live to please. They support God's vision by reminding us that we live to make God known and to demonstrate His unconditional love to all those around us. In essence, they capture our heart and compel us to action.

- Live the life of your dreams today.
- Success isn't enough—live for significance.
- Live for the audience of one.
- Be "His love extended" every day to everyone.
- Embrace the process.
- Success equals obedience.
- Value people. The person in front of us deserves our full attention.
- God created everyone on purpose and for a purpose.
- God always has our best interest at heart.
- Never settle for good. Reach for God's best.

AN INTENTIONAL APPLICATION
What mottos do you live by?

Take a few moments to consider and answer the following questions to create your own value statements: What quotes inspire you? What statements capture who you are in any given day? What mottos do you live by? Talk together and jot down your thoughts. They can be funny, serious, instructional, or inspirational. Think of the exercise like this: If you created a bumper sticker for your car to capture who you are, what would it say? If you could share a message with the world, what would that message be?

-
-
-
-
-
-

Don't worry about filling in a sentence by every bullet point. Simply write the mottos you adhere to and can identify at this point of life. Or, if you have more, feel free to add more bullet points to your list.

QUESTIONS TO CONSIDER
As a couple, what values do you share in common? Why are they important to you and your spouse? And how do they impact your decisions?

Your core values reveal who you are, and who you are determines how you do everything. The mottos you live by and embrace every day determine your actions. As you build on common values and define the life mottos you share as a couple, you continue to build common ground. With your mottos and values in place, let's uncover additional areas of common interest. After all, the passions you share in common, when aligned with God, lead you toward your marriage purpose.

> A Thought from T. D. Jakes
> *If you can't figure out your purpose, figure out your passion. For your passion will lead you right into your purpose.*[18]

When our middle daughter Sommer turned six years old, she asked, "Mommy, which do you want me to do? Should I do dance or do cheerleading?" Ironically, at the time, Julie faced a quandary herself. Much like Sommer, she faced a decision of what she should do. For weeks she sought God, poring over her list of duties and opportunities. Everything on the list seemed important. She felt stuck and kept asking God the same question that Sommer had asked her: *Which do You want me to do?* Her answer came in her response to Sommer. "Baby doll, which would you enjoy the most?"

As parents, we want our kids to enjoy what they do. Likewise, God desires us to enjoy life to its fullest. Sometimes, we complicate our purpose, mulling over lists, fearing we will miss God's voice or mess up His purpose. We agonize over God's will and what He wants when most of the time He's simply responding, *Which would you enjoy the most?* Our passions lead us to our purpose. They identify unique qualities of our design.

Take a moment to complete the following survey. Go to our website at www.MarriedforaPurpose.com/resources and print two copies of the survey, one for each of you. Fill in the surveys independently. Once you've done that, compare your lists. Then record the interests you share in common on a separate piece of paper. Later, you'll use this list of your shared common interests to answer to this chapter's study guide questions.

***

Common Interests Survey

SPIRITUAL ACTIVITIES
__ Administration
__ mentoring/discipleship
__ Attending retreats
__ Attending Conferences
__ Community outreaches
__ international outreaches
__ Bible Studies
__ Prayer/intercession
__ Teaching Adults
__ Teaching Children
__ Preaching
__ Worshiping
__ Writing
__ Singing
__ leading
__ encouraging
__ hospitality
other_____

ACTS OF SERVICE
__ Business
__ Caring for infants
__ Cooking
__ Cleaning
__ Greeting
__ media/videography
__ Photography
__ restoring Things
__ decorating
__ Planning
__ organizing
__ Painting
__ fixing Broken Things
__ Building
__ Plumbing
__ roofing
__ feeding the hungry
other_____

SPORTS
__ Softball
__ Swimming
__ Golf
__ Tennis
__ Cycling
__ Working out
__ volleyball
__ Basketball
__ Biking
__ running
__ Walking
__ Aerobics
__ Canoe/Kayaking
__ hiking
__ Caving
__ Surfing
__ Snorkeling
other_____

OTHER INTERESTS
__ Painting
__ dancing
__ reading
__ drawing
__ Traveling
__ Being outdoors
__ fishing
__ hunting
__ designing
__ Playing an instrument
__ Watching movies
__ music
__ Art
__ history
__ Shopping
__ decorating
__ Graphic design
other_____

WHAT'S OUR COMMON GROUND?

You are making great progress and are well on your way to discovering God's purpose for your marriage. So far you've pinpointed your core values; you've defined your life mottos and checked areas of common interests. Now it's time to consider your *who*.

AN INTENTIONAL APPLICATION
Define whom you both like to serve or serve alongside.

Together, take a moment to discuss whom you care about. Is there a particular group of people you both feel passionate to help or serve (i.e., family, local community, youth, adults, believers, unbelievers, influencers, leaders, businesses, churches, women, men, families, children, your nation, other nations, individuals who've been sex-trafficked, addicts, the homeless, the rich, the poor, etc.)?

Your *who* directs your focus. For example, a lot of people like to write. Some use their imagination to write fictional stories to motivate people to action; others write stories for entertainment, while some others write manuscripts filled with how-tos. Whom each of those writers cares about affects how they write. If children, it may be with cartoon characters to unfold a life lesson. If teens, the animation changes—the voice requires more everyday language. If the writer's heart tends toward the highly educated, again the language modifies to fit that audience. Although you may not be a writer, you still have a *who*. In other words, just like our values shape who we are and who we are determines how we do everything, then whom we care about shapes our message and how we communicate. Whom we care about channels our focus and determines where we spend our energy.

As a couple, you may care about many noble causes, but whom do you care about the most and whom do you feel the most equipped to help? For example, we both care about sex-trafficked victims, we care about the hungry, and we care about spreading the name of Jesus to the unchurched areas of our world. But when we look at our life experience and whom we feel the most passionate about, equipped, and gifted to help, we understand *whom* our *who* is. Our *who* are couples—we care about marriage and family. As a result, we spend the majority of our time and energy focusing on couples, and thus we use our talents to help families build strong, healthy relationships.

As a couple, who is your *who*? Answer the following questions in order to help you better determine:

1. Whom do you most enjoy being around?
2. Is there a particular group you both love to help?
3. Whom do you naturally find yourself reaching out to?

Let's begin to tie this all together. Set aside time to talk through the study guide questions of this chapter.

Study Guide: Chapter 6

Questions to Consider

1. How can you ensure you honor your core values and keep them at the forefront of your decision making?
2. What similar passions do you share?
3. How are your talents and gifts similar?
4. Whom or what groups of people do you both care about the most?
5. Make a list of one another's strengths and share what you admire about one another.
6. Share with one another your answers to the following sentences:
   - We enjoy...
   - We feel most useful when we...
   - In a crowd we feel most comfortable...
   - People frequently seek our help to...
   - We serve most naturally, with the least amount of effort, when we...
7. Discuss your answers to the following questions: What do we love doing? What brings us joy? What would we do even if we never got paid for it?

Scriptures to Study

- Mark 3:24
- Acts 18:18, 26, 42–47
- Romans 16:3–4
- 1 Corinthians 16:19–20

A Simple Prayer

Father, help us to build on common ground and not waste our energy trying to compete or compare our gifts with one another. Help us to live out our core values and life mottos in such a way that others are drawn to You through our marriage. We don't want to fight against one another; we want to fight for Your purpose and make a difference in this world. Help us to use our gifts and talents to honor You in all we do as we live out Your purpose together. Amen.

Chapter 7

WHAT FUELS OUR PURPOSE?

A Timeless Truth
Envisioning our ideal marriage and God's purpose for it fuels us to become all He intended.

Now that you've welcomed your differences, at least on most days, and defined your core values, common interests, and whom you feel most passionate to help, it's time to answer the next important question: What do you want for your marriage?

No, seriously though: What do you *really* want for your marriage? In your most perfect vision, what does your marriage relationship look like? If you're like most people, answering that question may take a few minutes, which we encourage you to do. After all, our best answers often bury themselves beneath more familiar answers that are concerned with what others expect from or desire for our marriage. In other words, we are *not* asking what your parents, kids, or pastor want for your marriage; we're not asking what you *want to want* or what you *know you should want* for your marriage; we're not even talking about what you feel *obligated to provide* for your marriage. We're simply asking, as a couple, what do you really want for your marriage? When's the last time you intentionally set aside time to dream together as a couple?

In *The 7 Habits of Highly Effective People,* Dr. Stephen Covey writes, "Begin with the end in mind. Envision what you want in the future so that you know concretely what to make a reality."[1] When asked, most couples say they want to live full-on for God's purpose—they want to begin with the end in mind. But more often than not, they find themselves stuck wondering, *How do we know if our vision aligns with God's vision?* They hold back from embracing their dream out of a fear it may not be spiritual enough.

Isn't it easy to allow the fear of missing God's purpose or mistaking it with our own to keep us from dreaming? Isn't it easy, amidst life's difficulties, to forget God is for us and that He desires good things for our life? From the time we're little we're taught that God's ways are higher than our ways, and that His thoughts are higher than our thoughts,[2] and, though that's absolutely true, we often forget to balance that truth with other Scriptures that remind us:

- The same Spirit that raised Christ from the dead now lives in us,[3] so we can rest knowing that God's Spirit will empower and guide our thoughts to align with His.
- He will put His Spirit in us to teach us in the way we should go.[4] We can take comfort that His Spirit will correct us and convict us if we get off track.
- We possess the mind of Christ,[5] and when we seek Him first in all things He gives us the desires of our heart[6]—our very passions, when surrendered to our Creator, actually come from Him. Those passions and the dream you already envision for your marriage reveal His purpose.

Greg says, "That should make you want to jump up and give your spouse a chest bump." Julie thinks a quick high five may be more appropriate. Either way, knowing God already empowered you with His vision and equipped you to accomplish His big idea should inspire you to dream big together.

Envisioning our ideal marriage and God's purpose for it fuels us to become all He intended for us to be. Like Joseph, the clearer we envision God's purpose, the more determined we press through life's difficulties in order to obtain it.

A Discovery from God's Word

> The Lord was with Joseph and gave him success in whatever he did.[7]

"You'll never guess what I dreamed again last night," Joseph announced, as he naively skipped past his brothers' growing hostility.

Oh my word, there he goes again, Reuben thought as he rolled his eyes and went back to eating his honey and oats.

"C'mon. Guess." Joseph raised his eyebrows, excited to share all the details. His enthusiasm only fueled his brothers' escalating enmity.

Somebody please shut this pompous pip-squeak's mouth, Simeon thought as he looked to his father, who only seemed to share Joseph's enthusiasm. *I wish Father would send him out to feed the sheep or something. The annoying squirt needs a dose of humility!*

Levi looked up from the table and for a brief moment thought, *I honestly think if given the chance, I could kill you.*

Oblivious to his brothers' deepening hatred, Joseph tightened his new colorful robe around him and leaned into his father's arms. He deepened his voice to project his vision. "Just like the night before, we were binding sheaves of grain out in the field when suddenly my sheaf rose and stood upright, while your sheaves gathered around mine and bowed down to it—only this time the sun and moon and eleven stars were bowing down to me."[8]

Dan, Asher, and Issachar all looked up from their breakfast and shook their heads, completely infuriated. One by one they began shouting: "Do you intend to reign over us? Will you actually rule us?" Naphtali slammed his bowl against the table and left without saying a word.

Israel looked at Joseph's older brothers and recognized he needed to intervene, and intervene quickly. In an attempt to defuse his sons' anger, Israel, laughing robustly, turned to Joseph. "What is this dream you had? Will your mother and I and your brothers actually come and bow down to the ground before you?"[9] Then he said, "My, my Joseph, you have quite the imagination. But there is no time for play; time to work, boys." With that, Israel sent Joseph's older brothers to graze the flocks.

After his brothers left, Joseph asked, "Father, why do my brothers hate me? What did I say? Is it my fault that God gave me a dream?"

Israel reminisced of his own childhood ambitions and rivalry with his brother, Esau. "Don't worry, Son," he said. "God has a way of working out things like this. You'll see." Israel winked to comfort Joseph. "However, going forward, let's keep those dreams between the two of us—okay?"

Later that day, in an effort to make amends, Israel sent Joseph to Shechem. But instead of reconciliation, Joseph's brothers plotted against him: "Here comes that dreamer!" they said to each other. "Come now, let's kill him and throw him into one of these cisterns and say that a ferocious animal devoured him. Then we'll see what comes of his dreams."[10] Thus began the testing of Joseph's dream.

Can you imagine? God gives you a dream, but instead of ruling and reigning you're thrown into an empty cistern, sold into slavery, wrongfully accused by your master's spouse, and then sentenced to a life of imprisonment?

Maybe you can imagine. Oh, not necessarily being thrown into a pit or sold into slavery, but you live with the shattered hopes of not experiencing what you once envisioned for your marriage. You imagined sharing your dreams with your spouse into the wee hours of the morning, endless days filled with laughter, the joy of a lifelong teammate. Instead, your midnight conversations may have turned into midnight confrontations. Your endless days of laughter, challenged by your consuming debt and your endless to-dos. Your lifelong teammate became more like a lifelong cellmate, with neither of you feeling capable to press together toward God's promises for your marriage.

Over time our circumstances can rob us of the joy God intended. We start disqualifying our dreams based on those circumstances and feel powerless to grab hold of the destiny God designed for our marriage. Surely Joseph could relate. Surely he questioned his dream. Surely he wondered, "How did I miss God?" Or speculated, "I thought God designed me for a place of leadership; instead, I am forgotten, abandoned by those I love."

God's vision—His purpose—for your marriage will be tested. Beginning with the end in mind and clearly envisioning your marriage purpose provides the fuel to fulfill it. God's clear picture for your marriage empowers you in your quest for significance to never succumb to the shallow pursuit of importance.

> **A Thought from John C. Maxwell**
> *Once you taste significance, success will never satisfy you again.*[11]

Understanding God's vision for you and your spouse helps you to never diminish your purpose to artificial definitions of success. Instead, it offers a target to shoot for and a destination to arrive at. God calls us to pursue Him, and, as we pursue Him, He directs us and fills us with His passions.

THE QUESTION
Does your and your spouse's vision align with God's vision?

For most couples, when adversity strikes it's easy to begin doubting the authenticity or the orientation of their purpose. It's all the give, share, and lead kind of commands, challenged by life's curve balls that leave us questioning: Did we really hear from God? Does our vision for our marriage really align with His? Did we conjure up some noble notion and completely misinterpret God's purpose? The most effective servants have always been refined by fire. Something happens amidst God's fire: Character develops. Selfishness dies. And, on the other side of adversity, we simply point back to who God is and how He fulfilled His promises amidst our pain. Humility chokes out pride as God develops His likeness to radiate from us. Many times we will experience testing in the areas we feel the most passionate about and experience loss before we witness victory.

> A Thought from Rick Warren
> *There is no growth without change, no change without fear or loss, and no loss without pain.*[12]

Loss Before Victory

Sam and Trish knew God directed them to help their neighbor, Morgan, a single mom, reroof her home. When Sam learned of his company's downsizing and that his position would no longer be needed, God's direction was tested. Instead of caving in to fear, Sam and Trish committed to follow through. Thankfully, before they could even transfer funds to pay for Morgan's new roof, Sam received a call to interview for his dream job.

Genny and Paul wonder how they'll impart long-lasting wisdom to their youth group when their own twenty-two-year-old son openly announced he wasn't sure God existed. Instead of giving up or giving in, instead of hiding under guilt or shame, Genny and Paul continue to pour their lives into their son and their youth group. They seek prayers from everyone they know and continue to lovingly support their son as he navigates this season of his life. They didn't receive an immediate answer to their prayer; instead, they stand believing in God's Word, trusting that the truths they taught their son will not depart from him.[13]

Success Is Measured by Obedience

Shortly after God led us to build a national ministry, we underwent a difficult season. We lived in three different states within an eleven-month time frame. Our financial income reduced to 10 percent of what we'd been accustomed to making. To say our dream or vision was tested is a gross understatement.

One of the first things God called us to do was to share our testimony with a thousand people. At first, that sounded pretty awesome; unfortunately, at the time, however, no one sought us to speak at their meetings. Yet the intensity to share our testimony only grew. As we prayed, God conveyed the vision of what to do next. We typed our testimony on a sheet of paper and delivered it to a thousand mailboxes in the middle of a snowstorm. Determined of God's direction, we couldn't wait to witness the response. We waited in eager anticipation. And waited. And then waited some more. After three weeks of no response, we felt absolutely foolish and convinced we'd misunderstood God. In complete embarrassment we asked God to forgive us: *God, we are so sorry. Here we attributed Your name to something You obviously never called us to.* But before we could finish our prayer, God interrupted and filled our minds with this thought: *I never called you to be successful. I called you to be obedient. Well done.*

God measures success through obedience. No, we aren't recommending recklessly attributing God's name to selfish ambitions or haphazardly blundering forward with a well-God-told-me-to attitude; instead, we firmly believe that as we yield our heart and mind to Him, we can trust that He will give us the desires of our heart. So unless our desires contradict His Word or are in some way sinful, we can embrace the idea that God put those desires in our heart to begin with. We simply need to align our life to follow after Him and trust the results to Him.

> **A Thought from Brother Lawrence**
> *God never fails to show us the right way to go, as long as our only goal is to please Him and show our love for Him.*[14]

When you seek God with all your heart to discern the real vision of your perfect marriage, what you *really* want for your marriage complements your differences, builds upon common ground, and aligns with God's plan for your marriage.

Living the Dream

A few years back, as we talked about our ministry goals, Julie shared, "I feel like God promised we'd touch at least a million souls during our lifetime." She beamed as she thought of the possibilities. Then, as if some buzzkilling fear mongrel strolled into the room, her expressions turned from elation to bewilderment, "But I don't know how..." The reality of our circumstances overtook the hope God promised.

We were as broke as a joke, barely making ends meet. As mentioned earlier, we moved across the country and lived in three states within a single year. Influence was a privilege of our past. No one was lining up to hear our story. There were no book contracts. Opportunities to speak were scarce to say the least.

As our conversation continued, however, we decided to take a different approach. Rather than trying to figure out how we'd accomplish it, we imagined what we wanted and what we believed God desired.

We dreamed of speaking to several thousand people at a time, we envisioned being best-selling authors, and we felt the joy of standing on stages sharing our story, helping millions of people. We stayed in that thought for over an hour and we talked about how awesome it felt. Did you catch that? We talked about how it *felt*, not how it *would* feel. For a few uninterrupted glorious moments we lived our dream and loved the feeling. It felt life-giving.

> A Thought to Ponder
> *When God whispered His promise to you in the past, He already saw it in its full completion.*

Together, we spoke God's vision for our marriage in real time, as if it already were. Then we asked a different question. Rather than asking, "How do we get there?" we asked, "How did we get here?" The answers differed completely from before. Instead of we have to get this or we'll have to somehow do that, we envisioned the resources we already possessed and the steps we already took. We immediately knew our next steps and felt fueled by our vision to accomplish them.

> A Thought from John C. Maxwell
> *Clarity of vision creates clarity of priorities.*[15]

The quality of an answer is determined by the quality of the question. You see, when we ask questions like, How do we get there? or, What do we need to do in order to accomplish this? it causes us to think with a bottom-to-top mentality. We consider every struggle we'll encounter and we see every obstacle standing in our way. We feel overwhelmed before we even start the journey. But when we ask how we got here or how we accomplished it, we stop focusing on the obstacles and think from a position of overcoming. We no longer live problem focused but purpose focused in our approach. We see our dream, and the clarity of our vision shows us what we need to prioritize in order to seize God's dream for our marriage.

It may take a little practice to recondition your thought patterns and exercise your imagination, but with God's help you can do this. Make sure to keep Him at the center of every thought. Invite Him to reveal His purpose and He will.

> A Thought from Jim Loehr and Tony Schwartz
> *To build capacity, we must push beyond our normal limits, training in the same systematic way that elite athletes do.*[16]

In their *New York Times* best-seller *The Power of Full Engagement,* Jim Loehr and Tony Schwartz share, "We build emotional, mental and spiritual capacity in precisely the same way that we build physical capacity."[17] Just as you exercise to strengthen your physical muscles, you can condition your thoughts to align with God's thoughts—the One whose thoughts are higher than your own, the One who sees His promise in its fulfillment. In Psalm 139, David writes, "My frame was not hidden from you when I was made in the secret place. When I was woven together in the depths of the earth, your eyes saw my unformed body. All the days ordained for me were written in your book before one of them came to be."[18] God in His infinite omnipotence sees our life from beginning to end.[19] Unbound by time, space, or circumstances, God makes His plans known for our life. Thus, seeking Him and submitting our thoughts to Him through prayer is essential.

A Deeper Look at Scripture

How should we pray? In Matthew, Jesus teaches, "This, then, is how you should pray: 'Our Father in heaven, hallowed be your name, your kingdom come, your will be done on earth as it is in heaven.'"[20] Whoa, whoa, whoa! Think about Jesus' instructions here. What did He mean by praying "your kingdom come, your will be done on earth as it is in heaven"? Have you ever stopped to consider how God's will takes place in heaven?

God's will in heaven is unhindered. It knows no constraint. In heaven, there is no pride of who gets the glory or who gives the order. In heaven, when God speaks it's already done. Here on earth, we simply need to align our life to follow after it. The more you practice thinking from God's perspective, unhindered, with no constraints, and live under His authority, the clearer vision you'll gain. The clearer the vision you gain, the greater perspective you'll acquire to make the decisions necessary to live out His purpose for your marriage. But it all starts with a clear vision under God's authority.

AN INTROSPECTIVE CHALLENGE
What do you dream about together?

What do you want for your marriage? Let's say five years from now, what does your marriage look like? What do you and your spouse do? If you have kids, what are they doing? Where do you live? What kind of income do you enjoy? How do you serve together? How do you honor one another? Use your imagination and think forward.

> A Thought from Napoleon Hill
> *There's a difference between wishing for a thing and being ready to receive it. No one is ready for a thing, until he believes he can acquire it. The state of mind must be belief, not mere hope or wish.*[21]

Dreaming Together

Our friend Ed DeCosta, a renowned executive coach, shares the following exercise. Imagine being handed a DVD, and the label on the DVD reads Highlights of Your Life with a date marked five years from today.

AN INTENTIONAL APPLICATION
Take a moment to describe what's on your marriage DVD.

For the purpose of discovering your marriage vision, take a moment to describe your future together. What does it look like? What is God's perfect vision for you and your spouse? What does it look like five years from today? What passions are you sharing in common? How do you demonstrate love to one another? How is your health? How do your values align with that vision? How are your differences strengthening one another to fulfill that vision? Furthermore, what kind of income are you sharing? Where do you live? Whom do you serve?

Maybe it is something like, *We are healthy, we make an income of _____, we live in _____, our home has bedrooms and a pool out back. We appreciate mornings together drinking coffee while enjoying the lake view in our back yard. We are happy because we have lots of friends whom we love to entertain and cook for on the weekends. Our home offers a place of peace for those who need it, as well as for ourselves. It's comfortable and people enjoy visiting because they feel God's love.*

Seriously, what do you see? How are you truly serving? Does it seem real? Don't fabricate your story with wishful thinking; instead, examine God's purpose and vision for your marriage and ask, Can we really envision living this life together? Behind the vision follows a knowing.

WHAT FUELS OUR PURPOSE?

Joseph knew God gave him a dream. When you know God gave you the dream, you'll be better able to live in such a way that you align your life to follow after it. Listen to what He's speaking to your spirit at this very moment. Dream together with your eyes wide open.

> A Thought from T. E. Lawrence
> *All men dream but not equally. Those who dream by night in the dusty recesses of their minds awake to the day to find it was all vanity. But the dreamers of the day are dangerous men, for they may act out their dreams with open eyes, to make it possible.*[22]

John and Mary envision living in a mobile camper and traveling around the US to visit their kids, sharing how God healed their marriage. Tracey and Ben foresee adopting three orphans from Africa—they live the dream every day and make necessary financial sacrifices to prepare for their children's arrival. Tonya and Mitch finished out their basement to live their marriage purpose. Their home now houses Tonya's aging mother in the upstairs spare room. Their basement houses Tonya's eldest daughter, son-in-law, and two grandsons. Both remain committed to being a haven of rest and a home of hospitality to all who need shelter. Though it comes with its challenges, they enjoy it.

As you describe the highlights on your proverbial DVD, you're thinking from a higher level of thought than most ever embrace. You're actually creating a vision for your marriage and envisioning the life you desire to create together. And that's even better than a goal, because it's real and it's attainable. You can see God's vision and you can feel the emotions and smell the air of your future life together.

Consider any other areas you need to explore. Allow God's perfect vision to fuel your imagination. Live that life. Embrace that perfect marriage with your spouse. The key is to feel how it feels to be living it. "You must see it to seize it!"[23]

AN INTENTIONAL APPLICATION

Using your imagination, ask: How did we get here? How did we accomplish it? What kinds of activities did we participate in to arrive where we arrived? What kinds of decisions and principles governed our life?

Remember that it may take a little practice, but as with any exercise you grow stronger, right? The same stands true with your imagination. The more you practice, the clearer you'll embrace God's purpose for your marriage. The more you align your life to follow after Him and His promise, the more you bring His vision to life. And we know that the more you bring His vision to life and live in it, the more your life and your marriage thrives.

Study Guide: Chapter 7

Questions to Consider

1. Continue to share ideas together of what you believe God's purpose is for your marriage.
2. Talk about ways you can serve and live the vision of your marriage. Begin to jot down your ideas—you'll need them for the next chapter.
3. How do you see yourself serving most naturally, both now and in the future?
4. What are you most excited about concerning your future together?
5. Take a moment to further define whom and what you care about.

Scriptures to Study

- Genesis 37:9–20
- Psalm 32:8; 37:4
- Isaiah 55:8–9
- Matthew 9:9–10
- John 14:26
- Romans 8:11
- 1 Corinthians 2:16

A Simple Prayer

Father, we never want to attribute Your name to something You haven't called us to. We also don't want to miss out on anything You have planned or purposed for our marriage. Inspire us to dream

Study Guide: Chapter 7

big. Awaken passions that align with Your vision for our marriage. Teach us whom to serve, what You desire from us, and how to live out Your perfect design for our marriage. Encourage and equip us to do what You've called us to do. Empower us to live in Your perfect plan.

Chapter 8

HOW DO WE DEFINE OUR PURPOSE?

A Timeless Truth
Articulating God's design for your marriage
provides clarity and direction for your relationship.

don't you just love Billy Graham? Billy Graham spent the majority of his life upholding a singular vision—leading sinners to the Savior. His relentless vision to seek and to save the lost consumed his thoughts and captured his affections. He understood that good is the enemy of great. Though given multiple opportunities, he resisted the temptation to build schools archiving his achievements. He abstained from expending his energy to organize feeding programs for the hungry or providing shelters for orphans.
Billy understood that although these projects were noble and necessary, they would distract him from God's purpose for his life.
Today, we celebrate Billy Graham as a man who embraces God's exact design for his life. We honor him because of his ability to live with an unwavering clarity and unswerving simplicity to seek and save that which was lost.

Articulating God's design for your marriage provides clarity and direction for your relationship. Many times couples hesitate to document God's vision for their marriage and wonder, *Is this big enough? Is this too big? How do we truly write out our vision, concisely, and know we landed on the right vision?* If you're feeling the same, hold on a minute. Don't break out in a cold sweat.

Rather, know this. You will likely continue to gain clarity on your marriage purpose for the rest of your life. Though your marriage purpose doesn't typically change, your understanding of it will. After all, Billy Graham didn't know every detail of his journey when he first began. The key to defining your marriage purpose rests in capturing a broad enough description to encompass the fullness of who you are as a couple, while providing a clear enough description to eliminate distractions. Either way, don't allow what you don't know to trap you from establishing what you do know.

> A Thought from John C. Maxwell
> *The greatest mistake we make is living in constant fear that we will make one.*[1]

In the last chapter you spoke your marriage vision out loud; now it's time to write it down—a practice God commanded to Habakkuk in the seventh century BC.

A Discovery from God's Word

> Then the Lord replied: "Write down the revelation and make it plain on tablets so that a herald may run with it."[2]

Devastated but determined, Habakkuk climbed atop Judah's highest tower overlooking its border. Something in his spirit shouted, *I will not leave this place until I gain understanding. Pity the man who tries to tear me from this spot before I hear from God.*

It'd been an exhausting season. Habakkuk faced inevitable changes and even more challenges. His people lived divided, broken into factions, and remained scattered across the countryside.

Judah faced one of the bleakest moments in Israel's history. The Babylonian Empire threatened to invade and carry away God's people into captivity. It wasn't looking too good for the home team. Overcome by grief, fear pressed Habakkuk to speak words he'd normally never dare utter. After all, he was a prophet. Prophets were supposed to know answers to life's problems. But circumstances tested Habakkuk's resolve and tried his faith. *I'm not trying to complain, Lord, but I don't understand any of this. You promised to bless Your people. You promised to give them hope and a future, but instead Babylon is about to enslave us.*

Habakkuk felt like we often feel when God whispers a promise to us, but instead of experiencing it, we endure a season of testing. What then? How do we press on? How do we move forward? How do we persevere toward God's purpose for our marriage when obstacles seem like they're going to overtake us?

Habakkuk clenched his fists tightly to the side of his head and yelled at the top of his lungs, "I will not leave here until I hear from You, God. I am not moving from this spot until You give me direction." And then, at just the right moment, as if lightning flashed against the horizon and lifted a veil of darkness, God revived Habakkuk with a solution and whispered a simple instruction that promised to help the prophet run with perseverance.

What did God speak? What nugget offered Habakkuk so much promise? What would help him run steadily, regardless of the opposition he faced along the way? It's the same exercise you're about to undertake. God said, "Write down the revelation and make it plain on tablets so that a herald may run with it."[3]

Why do we write down our purpose? It's so that we can persevere.

Every couple encounters seasons of difficulty and experiences moments when God's dream and purpose for their marriage is tested. By writing down God's vision, we gain a greater understanding to truly know our purpose. The more we know our marriage purpose, the more conviction we gain to live it. And the more conviction we hold, the better we run toward it, persevering regardless of opposition. Writing down our marriage purpose serves as a memorial to awaken hope during every season of life, and it acts as a beacon to keep us on course, which is something God tells His people to do time and time again.

A Deeper Look at Scripture

Several times throughout Scripture God commands His servants to write and record His words. In Exodus 17:14, God said to Moses, "Write this on a scroll as something to be remembered and make sure that Joshua hears it." And in Exodus 34:27, God says, "Write down these words, for in accordance with these words I have made a covenant with you and with Israel." When God appeared to Jeremiah, He told him to "write in a book all the words I have spoken to you."[4] In Revelation 21:5, God spoke to John, saying, "I am making everything new!" Then he said, "Write this down, for these words are trustworthy and true."

Are you getting it? It seems that every time something was to be remembered, God's servants wrote it down. God Himself demonstrates His love and commitment by inscribing us on the palms of His hands.[5] Wow! God found you worthy to be inscribed. He believed in you and found you so valuable and precious that He carved you on the palms of His hands. You and your spouse are remembered. What do you find worthy to be remembered? What is God inspiring you to write down? Defining His vision for your marriage will empower you to live it out in your day-to-day life.

We once heard the late Zig Ziglar share that only 3 percent of people ever write their goals down, but 97 percent of those people achieve them. In fact, anyone who teaches on achievement, success, or living your dream encourages you to document your goals.

If you don't write down your goals, they become moving targets based on circumstances; thus, writing down your ultimate goal for life—living God's purpose for your marriage—proves vital.

What should you write down? How do you record the purpose God has entrusted to you and to your spouse? How do you commemorate His specific purpose for your marriage? That is what we're about to reveal. So let's jump into uncharted waters to document the singular purpose God destined for you and your spouse, so that, like Billy Graham, you move forward through life with laser-focused clarity and unswerving simplicity to lay claim of God's purpose together.

THE QUESTION
How do we define our purpose?

As mentioned in previous chapters, our passions ultimately serve as a compass to discover our purpose. At this point, we hope to help you capture and condense the conversations you've already discussed about those passions since beginning this book. You may find it useful to gather your written notes and lists from previous exercises to ensure you seize every thought and secure your discoveries.

You'll notice you've already discussed many of the following questions, but now it's time to summarize those conversations in written form and encapsulate them in one central location. Keep in mind that you'll use the following applications to construct a singular statement that describes and clarifies your marriage purpose in order to memorialize it.

Gather Perspective
Take a few moments to succinctly write your answers to the following questions. (You may consider reviewing your notes and

the lists constructed from chapter 6 to help express your thoughts more concisely.)

1. Write down what you love or enjoy doing together as a couple. Consider the areas of common activities you both enjoy from the survey in chapter 6. Write down your combined interests below.

2. When it comes to serving, describe ways you love to serve others together as a couple. Include common areas of strength, but don't overlook areas where your differences complement one another.

3. List ways you can use your passions to coincide with God's call. Be creative. Don't allow circumstances to limit you. What interests pique your passions as a couple and utilize your gifts for God together? Record your thoughts below.

4. Has God ever whispered a promise to you (from the Bible) that motivated you as a couple? If so, what did He whisper? If not, invite Him to reveal His design for your marriage. Think about this: If God sat before you right now, and you asked Him, "What do You desire for us to do together as a couple?" what would He say? How would He answer you? Take a moment to jot down what you believe God might be speaking to you or how He has already spoken.

AN INTROSPECTIVE CHALLENGE
Remember, God's design for you and your spouse is as unique as God is creative.

In Louisville, Kentucky, God surrounded us with extremely talented individuals and gave Julie the opportunity to build a women's ministry team. We loved watching the body of Christ in action. Jenni interceded like a true intercessor; Elizabeth oversaw details and made designs better; Billie loved helping people discover the spiritual gifts that God had given to them; and Heidi organized activities like spelunking and took women hiking and camping. Then there was Rose, who organized a book club for women, and Gina who facilitated Bible studies imploring women to a greater intimacy with God. Each woman utilized her passions, and, as a result, we witnessed several salvations, healings, and miracles. People who would never pass through the doors of our church building came to the saving knowledge of Jesus because each woman simply embraced her God-given interest and used her passions to share God's love.

The same holds true for you and your spouse too.

You play a role in God's kingdom. The expression of your gift is unique. God already designed you for it. You may not share Billy Graham's overt call to ministry, so don't waste time trying to figure out if your marriage purpose is spiritual enough. After all, Billy's call completely differs from our friend John Maxwell's. John lives to teach leadership principles and grow leaders around the world. He's written over one hundred books on leadership. As he faithfully uses his gifts, he also shares the love of Christ. One of John's greatest joys is leading people to Christ, but building leaders remains John's primary calling.

In the end, the tasks we are called to are not as important as our obedience to the One who calls us to them. In other words, John won't be held accountable for Billy's ministry, and neither will any of us be held accountable for another's purpose. We are only accountable for our own—what God has called each of us to do. So let's move forward and clearly document what that purpose/vision looks like as a couple.

Record Your Marriage Vision

In a few paragraphs, begin to record your marriage vision. Remember the DVD exercise? You've already talked about it at great length, but now it's time to write down what you've been dreaming about together. List as much detail as possible. Be sure to enter thoughts from the vision as discussed in chapter 7. Include whom you both desire to help, two or three passions you share in common with one another, and the activities that cause you to feel the most fulfilled.

HOW DO WE DEFINE OUR PURPOSE?

Remember to begin with the end in mind. Your content should address both of your *who, what, when, why,* and *how* as a couple:

- Whom do you care about?
- What do you love doing?
- When have you seen fruit from those gifts?
- Why do you feel inspired that this is God's purpose for your marriage?
- As you put pen to paper, think about your legacy—how do you want to be remembered as a couple?
- You may also list three or more talents that you share in common or the differences that complement and empower you to serve in a particular area.

Don't limit or edit what you're writing; rather, expand and list as many ideas as you can think of as a couple. If you need more room, grab an additional sheet of paper to capture your thoughts. Take your time and journal anything you've shared that might be important to convey God's fingerprint design for your marriage.

Before moving on, reread the paragraphs written above. Take a moment to highlight any words or sentences that best describe and capture who you are as a couple.

Centralize Your Thoughts

In this next exercise, we encourage you to centralize your thoughts into a present tense vision for your marriage. As you answer the following sentences, write down your thoughts, declaring what is and what will be. Your words should define your actions and express your passions. Choose strong verbs—words depicting actions (serve, build, construct, lead, create, teach, write, sing [see http://www.MarriedforaPurpose.com/resources

for more examples]). Along with your verbs, add nouns and descriptive adjectives or adverbs—words that best express your passions around desired results and for whom you care about (sustainable growth, life-transforming, freely, passionately, encouraging, youth, elderly, believers, women, men [see http://www.MarriedforaPurpose.com/two-are-better-than-one for more examples]). Share your answers with one another and then condense them into short and memorable written statements. Use the space below to compose your answers. You may need to use a separate sheet of paper before recording your final answers.

We live to...

We love to...

We are passionate about...

We won't stop until we...

Now go back through and highlight any recurring themes or descriptive words listed in the last activity. You should begin noticing an overlap in content between the activities. True themes will naturally emerge. The consistencies reveal what's most important to you and serve as clues to God's specific design for your marriage.

Providing Pathways of Growth

We believe God created us to provide pathways to sustainable growth and life transformation. That single purpose statement guides all of our decisions as a couple. It presents a picture of whom we involve in our life. We feel compelled to help people who want to grow, who want to leave a legacy and make a difference. When an opportunity presents itself, we know to ask one another, Will what we offer bring life to this organization or activity?

Our purpose to provide pathways holds us accountable to continually sharpen the way we interact and influences how much time we allow for a given project. It directs what we say yes to and what we say no to. It serves as our navigation system and keeps us on track to live our purpose. Our purpose statement keeps us from settling for what is good and inspires and disciplines us to live for what is great.

> A Thought from Jim Collins
> *Good is the enemy of great.*[6]

In his book *Good to Great*, Jim Collins writes, "Good is the enemy of great. And that is one of the key reasons why we have so little that becomes great.... Few people attain great lives, in large part because it is just so easy to settle for a good life."[7]

As created beings, our energy, creativity, and capacity is finite. To fully experience the infinite, we must abandon our inclination to settle for what is good and reach forward to hold fast to God, relentlessly pursuing the design He intended for our marriage. Remember, when you say yes to something you say no to something else. We've found that in order for us to live God's design for our marriage, we need to constantly examine whether or not we are adding value in a sustainable manner. We ask ourselves, Does this message or system promote pathways for individuals, couples, or businesses to grow? When parenting, we avoid the because-we-told-you-so philosophies; instead, we ask our kids self-reflective questions to promote discovery. We equip our kids by providing practical, spiritual, value-based principles they can apply to their lives. And, as our friend Paul Martinelli, president of the John Maxwell team, says, "Don't just teach them what to think; teach them how to think."

Honestly, at this point in our marriage journey, we can't help ourselves. Intentionality makes us tick. It's who we are. We love providing pathways that help others experience the aha moments of life. We feel burned out if we don't deliver something that truly influences change. We'd rather have our hairs plucked out one strand at a time or be forced to walk backward the rest of our lives than be confined to work with people who only want to live in their misery.

When we look back at previous chapters to evaluate our own purpose statement, it passes the test. We live the Great Commission in our home, in businesses, and in churches by lifting one another up and demonstrating value-based principles that honor Him and inspire others to live life as He desired — to its fullest. We don't thump people over the head with the Bible; instead, we strive to live by its principles. We hope to model it out in our life and marriage in such a way that others are drawn to the love God's given to us. Do you see how our purpose statement stands as the central part of everything we do? How it serves as a guide to keep us from settling for what might be good activities but not great activities for how God designed us?

Our passion is to truly bring God glory through proven systems that influence growth and sustainable life transformation. We live to love unconditionally and to help others do the same. It's who we are. It's what we do. It's the DNA God hardwired in us. What DNA did God put in you? What specific purpose did He design for your marriage?

Revisit Your Charts

In this final exercise, take a moment to reread what you've already written. Revisit your charts. Think about the recurring themes and passions you've discovered in previous exercises. Then talk together about what you believe God designed and called you to do. After talking and sharing together, write down your purpose concisely, in a couple of sentences or less.

(Again, our purpose is to provide pathways to sustainable growth and life transformation. We chose each word carefully to afford the most room of fully encompassing our passions and yet a narrow enough description to streamline our focus. *Pathways* might mean books, blogs, posts, lessons, study guides, or videos; it offers a wide range to encompass all of our passions. Yet *to sustainable growth* directs the focus of our creativity. We don't write to be cute. We don't produce videos to simply entertain. Stimulating growth and life transformation motivates everything we do.)

Don't worry if your purpose statement doesn't seem as refined—it will over time. Instead, as our friend Tammy Maltby says, "Start simply. But simply start." Begin developing your purpose statement by answering one of the following sentences. Write your thoughts on a separate sheet of paper and then narrow down your statement until you've condensed it to a maximum of twenty-one words. Then record your final answers.

If we could accomplish one thing in life together, it would be…

HOW DO WE DEFINE OUR PURPOSE?

The one thing we are confident God has called us to do is…

If you've followed and consistently completed each exercise, you've gained more clarity than most couples ever consider. Yahoo! Congratulations, because you have discovered what you've been searching for—your marriage purpose. Well done! But don't back off now. Some of the most important activities of living your purpose remain ahead in chapters 9 and 10.

Remember, you'll continue to gain clarity the rest of your life together, so let's take a moment to test your marriage purpose and make any necessary modifications. Consider the following questions located in the study guide and then pray together. Also we'd love to know what you discovered. Take a moment to share it with us online at www.MarriedforaPurpose.com. Maximize your dis- coveries by sharing your purpose statement with your pastor and small group.

Study Guide: Chapter 8

Questions to Consider

1. Does your vision statement support the three building blocks of living the Great Commission, bringing God pleasure, and demonstrating His unconditional love?

2. Does it inspire you to build a life together toward a common purpose?

3. Do you feel like God supports your vision through His Word, through the circumstances or experiences of your life, and do others validate it?

4. Does the vision allow opportunity for both of you to use your strengths and contribute to the overall dream?

5. Does your vision align with your core values of what you believe to be your most important qualities, attributes, and beliefs?

6. Do you envision a clear picture of whom you want to serve, how you want to serve, and why you want to serve? If not, make any changes necessary to help serve as a guidepost for the future.

7. When you think of your legacy and what you want to be remembered for, does the purpose you wrote down help you to fulfill that vision?

Scriptures to Study

- Deuteronomy 31:24
- Joshua 24:26
- Ecclesiastes 3:14
- Isaiah 42:16; 46:10
- Jeremiah 30:2
- Habakkuk 2:1–4

A Simple Prayer

Father, thank You for the vision You've given us as a couple. Help us to stay on the right path and honor one another first, and then honor others. Make our marriage strong. You designed us on purpose and for a purpose—help us to live fully in it.

Chapter 9
HOW DO WE PROTECT GOD'S PURPOSE?

A Timeless Truth
God doesn't need you to do anything for Him,
but He invites you to participate with Him.

Well, no doubt you're feeling pretty excited at this point in your journey. After all, you just created a purpose statement articulating the fingerprint of God's design for your marriage. You see more clearly now than ever before how the two of you fit together to fulfill God's purpose for your marriage. So go ahead and give each other a quick high five, a celebratory hug, and a great big kiss. But then, as our friend and mentor John C. Maxwell urges us, celebrate and get back to work.

Seriously. There's much to do. Now that you've discovered and described His purpose for your marriage, it's time to develop and actually put it into practice. Guard His vision for your marriage ferociously. Defend His purpose at all costs. Live intentionally.

> A Thought from W. Clement Stone
> *No matter how carefully you plan your goals, they will never be more than pipe dreams unless you pursue them with gusto.*[1]

Instead of living resigned, live your design. Pursue the design God destined for your marriage together. Pursue His purpose for your marriage with gusto. And who better to look to as an example of living with gusto than our Savior, Jesus Christ?

A Discovery from God's Word

> Let us fix our eyes on Jesus, the author and perfecter of our faith.... Consider him who endured such opposition from sinful men, so that you will not grow weary and lose heart.[2]

The crowds didn't wait for an invitation; instead, they jumped in, asking Jesus more questions, seeking more signs, looking for additional wonders, and...well, food. After all, Jesus already fed them once, so maybe He would do it again.

Jesus, however, never concerned Himself with gaining people's approval. Unlike the Pharisees of the day, Jesus didn't worry about keeping count of the number of people following Him. He didn't have an ego to feed; instead, He operated from a higher wisdom, understanding that mobs are fickle. The masses always tended to follow at a distance, seeking signs and wanting to be fed. Instead of trying to attract followers with the latest fads and fashions, Jesus lived for a greater ambition—His purpose. Because Jesus lived selflessly, He willingly communicated unabridged truths for the betterment of all who listened.

In the gospel of John, Jesus spoke to the masses:

> "I tell you the truth, you are looking for me, not because you saw miraculous signs but because you ate the loaves and had your fill. Do not work for food that spoils, but for food that endures to eternal life, which the Son of Man will give you. On him God the Father has placed his seal of approval." Then they

asked him, "What must we do to do the works God requires?"[3]

Isn't that the question we all ask when we grow tired of being just another brick in the wall, hungry to fulfill the greater purpose of our existence? When a bigger house or more money doesn't satisfy our souls, and we find ourselves wanting more and desiring to do more, we begin asking questions like: Why are we here, and What does God require of us?

Jesus quickly responds to the crowd's question in a twofold manner. He first points out that accepting Him is their only hope, for He is the bread of life, He is the hope of all humankind, and He alone grants eternal life. Jesus first establishes that before we do for Him we must be founded in Him. It's our being in Him that empowers our doing for Him. Secondly, Jesus points out what God requires, saying, "For I have come down from heaven not to do my will but to do the will of him who sent me."[4] Jesus shares this singular purpose repeatedly throughout the Gospels:

- He states, "By myself I can do nothing; I judge only as I hear, and my judgment is just, for I seek not to please myself but him who sent me."[5]
- He prays to the Father, "I have brought you glory on earth by completing the work you gave me to do."[6]
- Later, as the time approached for Jesus to ascend into heaven, we read how Jesus resolutely set His face toward Jerusalem. Jesus knew why He'd come. He knew His destiny. He understood His purpose. Instead of pleading for more time or trying to hide, Jesus marches to the very city and place He knows He'll be crucified, determined to not let anything stand in His way.[7]

Jesus' passion to live out the Father's purpose, to do His will, exemplifies the heart we must maintain in order to live God's purpose for our marriage. In our pursuit to fulfill our marriage purpose, we must live with Jesus' resolve and not seek our own will, but the will of Him who sends us. Our ambition must be to accomplish His work.

Thankfully, our marriage purpose is a bit more joyful than crucifixion. On the contrary, more times than not, as we look at our design, life experience, passions, and values, and become intentional about using them for the kingdom, living purpose focused remains the most fulfilling pursuit we will ever endeavor. After all, it's what God designed us to do.

When we do that, we fully live in His purpose for our marriage and enjoy life far greater than we ever imagined. Although we occasionally encounter challenges attempting to hold us back, we can manage against those challenges and position ourselves for success by planning in advance.

A Thought from Alan Lakein
Failing to plan is planning to fail.[8]

Rocks lie hidden ahead, right? No one experiences calm seas all of the time, do they? Of course not! So throughout this chapter we want to encourage you to make plans to navigate the rocks that you know lurk just beneath the surface. With a little preparation you and your spouse will live uninhibited for God's distinct purpose, standing strong regardless of life's currents, pursuing God's purpose with gusto, just like Jesus. Together, with a little intentional preparation, the responsibilities demanding your attention and the circumstances attempting to discourage your dreams will no longer consume your energy.

Take a moment to recognize we only fully enjoy a mountaintop experience because of what it took to scale it. Amidst difficult seasons, be courageous and hold fast to what you know. The clarity you gained from chapters 1 through 7 and then expressed in written form in chapter 8 laid the foundation to build the infrastructure necessary to live God's purpose for your marriage every day, regardless of your circumstances.

THE QUESTION
How do we protect God's purpose and live our marriage vision?

Determining Small Steps

Determine small measurable steps you can take to move toward your marriage purpose. Consider asking these general questions to better prepare, protect, and live out God's purpose for your marriage:

1. What threats hold the potential of leading us off course or distracting us from fulfilling our marriage purpose?
2. How can we safeguard against those threats?
3. How can we plan for success?
4. What daily and weekly practices do we need to establish to defend our purpose?
5. What intentional habits can we develop to move us toward our purpose?

Schedule Time for Reflection

In order to apply this to our lives, we must schedule time for reflection every day. Our friend, vice president of the John Maxwell team, Scott Fay writes, "Too many people just accept their lives rather than lead their lives."[9] As mentioned earlier in this chapter, don't resign to the status quo of life—live your design. Don't waste your life waiting for the big opportunity, the big breakthrough, and overlook the opportunities to live with influence today. Take a moment right now to schedule time together to connect and reflect. When can you both talk for a minimum of fifteen minutes daily? Schedule it. Put it on your calendar.

Consider for a moment the law of sowing and reaping. If you plant a kernel of corn, you reap corn; if you plant tomato seeds, you'll harvest tomatoes; and if you plant green beans, you reap green beans. In other words, you reap what you sow, which is why in Galatians God's Word encourages us: "Let us not become weary in doing good, for at the proper time we will reap a harvest if we do not give up."[10] As you meet together daily and take time for reflection, you *will* impact your results and influence your outcomes. Here are a few additional questions to ask during your time of reflection. As you answer these questions, focus exclusively on your marriage purpose:

1. Is what you are doing right now—the way you are living, the practices you are performing, the actions you are taking, and the decisions you are making—planting the right seeds for your desired harvest?
2. What are you doing right now that will help yield a favorable result?
3. What actions do you need to take today to help produce your desired outcome?
4. Are there any habits (weeds) threatening your desired crop that need to be uprooted and gotten rid of?
5. Have you made concessions, accepting what is good instead of living for what is great?

As a side note, you can apply this application to any area of life (parenting, finances, communication, intimacy, or connection). Pick a subject and then ask the same questions listed above for greater growth and connection.

Manage for What Is Best

Several years ago, as we visited dear friends, we witnessed the unravelling of their relationship. Their kids felt isolated and overlooked. As a couple, they felt disconnected and burnt out. It seemed hopeless. Their ambition to serve God and make an impact stole from every other area of their life. They'd neglected time with one another. They sacrificed and spent themselves on the altar of the urgent. It seemed everyone needed more and more of them.

The more they spent time helping others, the less time they made for one another and their children. Someone else's needs always seemed more important than their own. It wasn't a bad thing that they wanted to help others—their intents were noble. It wasn't evil for them to want to make a difference; they just lost sight of adding value to others in a manner that was healthy for their own family. Unfortunately, our friends' story isn't uncommon. Unless you clearly know God's purpose and maintain a clear vision of your nonnegotiables, it's easy to sacrifice what's great and settle for what is good.

AN INTENTIONAL APPLICATION
Decide what you need to manage for and what you need to manage against in order to live your marriage purpose with no regrets.

In order to live God's purpose, we must determine the seeds we need to plant and keep watered. Likewise, we need to discern the weeds—the practices, habits, or faulty beliefs—that threaten us from living God's purpose so that we can remove them.

A Thought from Scott Fay
Tearing out our weeds may not be sexy, but it's necessary. Weeds keep growing and stealing our energy until we remove them.[11]

Weeds show up in the way of fear, anger, bitterness, or resentment. Weeds may be unforgiveness, guilt, or shame. They may be found in bad habits like poor time management, self-sufficiency instead of living in God's sufficiency, focusing on the past, or living for a person's approval. A weed could even be living inside our comfort zone. Even people who don't consider themselves to have a green thumb understand that weeds choke out the main crop, and though they may be easy to identify, they aren't always easy to get rid of. They tend to sprout up time and time again. So let's capture your answers to the questions you discussed above, identifying the habits and practices that will yield favorable results and habits that need to be removed in order to live your marriage purpose.

> A Thought from Stephen R. Covey
> *Most of us spend too much time on what is urgent and not enough time on what is important.*[12]

For the last seventeen years, we've taught the law of sowing and reaping in business, parenting, and in relationships. We've taught couples the power of thought and encouraged them to believe the best about one another while reminding them that they gravitate toward what they contemplate. We've taught that what you feed grows and what you starve dies. As facilitators of the Paterson Life-Plan, we host retreats for individuals and couples who want to take a deeper dive into God's purpose for their life. During that two- or three-day retreat, we spend hours helping individuals and couples uncover their individual or marriage purpose. As we work with them, we are committed to helping them identify the things they need to manage for and the things they need to manage against in order to live out God's purpose.[13]

For the purpose of charting, we will use the terms *things to manage for* and *things to manage against* to capture the vast array of concepts couples have shared with us as we've taught all these principles. As a quick explanation, the things we manage for in life stimulate growth. These are the things in life we need to feed. They are the seeds we need to plant and keep watered. They move us toward our desired goals. If tended to consistently, they help produce an optimal outcome. They are life giving in nature, run consistent with our needs, and support God's vision for our marriage and life. If we do not manage for these things, they will get crowded out by the busyness of life and we take the risk that Stephen Covey alluded to, which is allowing the urgent to choke out what's most important.

The things we need to manage against are the hazardous habits we practice that often keep us from moving toward our ideal marriage purpose. These are the things we need to starve. They are the weeds that need to be pulled. If we fail to manage against these practices or habits or faulty beliefs, we will not accomplish God's purpose in our marriage. Keep in mind that weeds can sometimes at first glance appear noble, but in the end they keep you in your comfort zone and rob you from God's best in your marriage.

THINGS TO MANAGE FOR

- Time for meaningful Conversations daily
- Preferring one Another's Needs
- Consistent date Nights
- Sexual intimacy
- Believe the Best about one Another
- devising and Agreeing on a financial Plan
- Speaking Words of Affirmation
- Seeking God daily and listening Carefully
- Connecting intentionally with the Kids
- dreaming Together
- Time to relax
- Growing intentionally

THINGS TO MANAGE AGAINST

- Poor Time management
- People Pleasing
- Time on Social media
- Allowing the World's Beliefs to form ours
- focusing on the Past
- frivolous/impulsive/unwise Spending
- Complaining
- Needing the Approval of others
- Too many Activities for the Kids
- Negative Thoughts
- Busyness
- Poor Self-image

Thinking about your marriage purpose, what decisions or changes do you need to make to ensure you fulfill it together as a couple? Take a moment to list the things you need to manage for and things you need to manage against in order to live out God's purpose for your marriage. As a reminder:

1. Use the top of the chart to list the most important things you need to nurture in order to fulfill God's purpose for your marriage. Think of the things you need to manage for as the seeds you need to plant and keep watered. These are what you need to feed. Consider the following questions when filling in the left side of your chart: What opportunities do you need to say yes to in order to move toward your marriage purpose? What disciplines do you need to add? What will help you build and sustain God's plan for your marriage?

2. Use the bottom of the chart to identify the things you need to manage against. These are the weeds that need pulled. You'll need to guard against these in order to experience optimal results. If you don't de-weed these thoughts, habits,

or practices, you will not be able to fulfill God's vision for your marriage. Consider the following questions when filling in the right side of your chart: What current activities hinder you from fulfilling your marriage purpose? What habits do you need to remove? What could keep you from moving toward God's best for your marriage?

You may want to print out this chart and post it alongside your core value statements, life mottos, and marriage purpose statement. Revisit the lists often in order to better sustain God's purpose for your marriage.

THINGS TO MANAGE FOR

-
-
-
-
-
-
-
-

THINGS TO MANAGE AGAINST

-
-
-
-
-
-
-
-

Just as seeds need planting, weeds need pulling, and certain parts of plants need pruning, so we need to prune areas of life that may not necessarily be innately bad but may hinder us from living out our specific purpose. In order to protect God's purpose for our marriage, we must prune activities stifling our optimal growth.

Know Your Nonnegotiables

Several months ago we received a mind-blowing offer to minister to a large group of people on a consistent basis. At first blush, it seemed as if God had extended an awe-inspiring opportunity to share His message. The ministry was strong, vibrant, and reputable. They maintained an unbelievable outreach program to the nations and an even more tremendous vision for expansion. There was one huge problem, however: the opportunity collided with a couple of our core values and nonnegotiables. Their ultimate needs didn't completely align with our design. As you know, our marriage purpose is to provide pathways to sustainable growth and life transformation, and we accomplish that by creating content that inspires change. God called us to write books, to film videos, and to develop curriculum, especially aimed at couples. The position did not afford us the liberty to do those tasks.

We also operate from a core value of needing freedom to express our ideas, to minister to people all across the world, and to share value-based principles in a creative manner. Again, because of the needs of the ministry we would need to abandon those passions. Ultimately, the position was only being offered to one of us. Since God designed us to minister together, we knew we needed to decline. We firmly believe the message of this book, that two are better than one.

Accepting the position would have been unfair to the ministry and directly threatened the work God has entrusted to us. Knowing God's design and clearly articulating our nonnegotiables kept us from making the wrong decision. To others the position offered a dream of a lifetime, but for us it opposed God's ultimate purpose for our marriage, which is why this next exercise is so vital.

> AN INTENTIONAL APPLICATION
> **Don't allow what is good to get in the way of what is great. Define your negotiables and your nonnegotiables.**

To sustain God's purpose for your marriage, you need to clearly define your negotiables and your nonnegotiables. What are you unwilling to sacrifice? What are you unwilling to give up? For your next exercise, take a moment to clearly define and chart your nonnegotiables to each area of life. By doing so, you will be better prepared to say no to opportunities that compromise your marriage purpose. To stimulate your thoughts, read through the samples from our chart, talk together, and then dive in to capture yours.

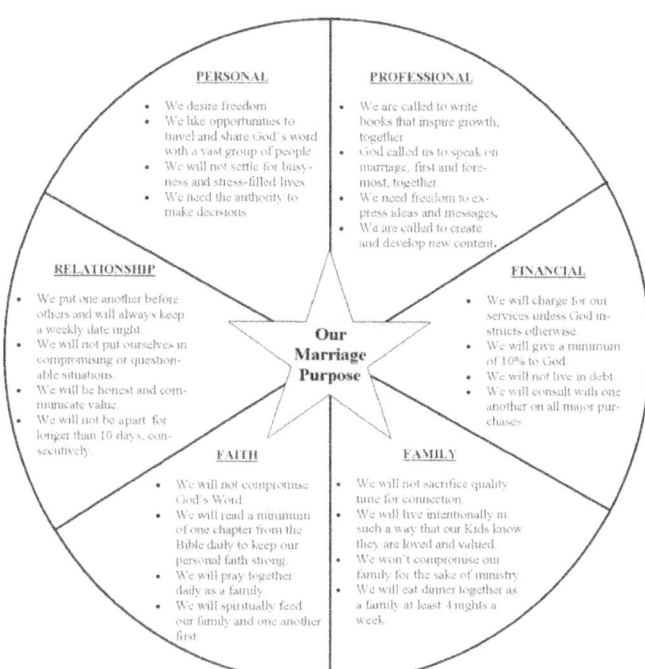

Now it's your turn. Go to www.MarriedforaPurpose.com/resources and print off the Nonnegotiable Chart. If you need a little help as you fill out this chart, consider the things you listed that you'll manage for and the things you'll manage against. Think about your vision of five years from now. What will you need to put into place in order to ensure its success and fulfillment? What will you need to guard at all costs if you want to be healthy—physically, emotionally, and spiritually? Consider beginning your nonnegotiable statements with phrases like, *We will* __ or *We won't* __. Try writing declarative sentences when possible. If wordsmithing doesn't come easy, consider listing two or three words that capture the essence of what yc

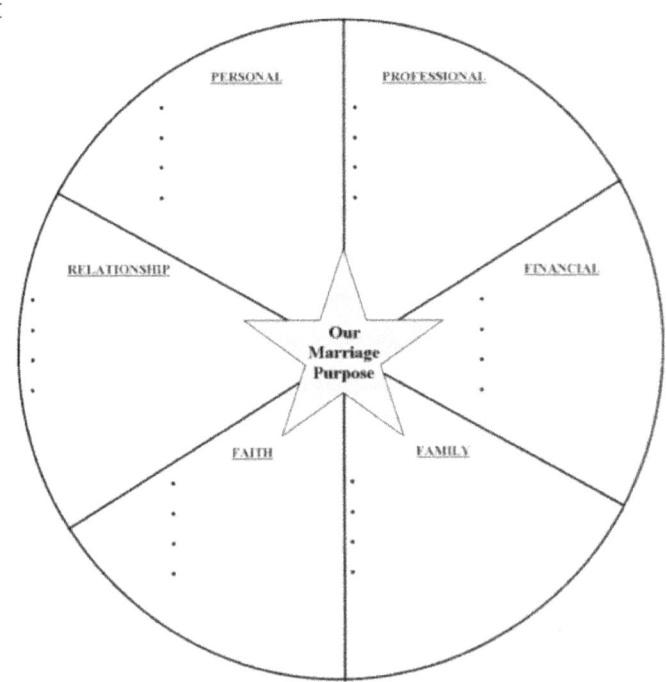

Before continuing to the final chapter, discuss your discoveries with your spouse. The study guide below includes questions to recap

your findings. And don't forget to celebrate all your hard work.

Study Guide: Chapter 9

Questions to Consider

1. What are some next-step, immediate actions you can take to pursue your marriage purpose with gusto?

2. What seeds do you need to plant or manage for right now?

3. What weeds need pulled or managed against today?

4. Have you made concessions, allowing what is good to get in the way of what is great? If so, what steps can you take to change that?

5. What nonnegotiables are you most excited about protecting together?

Scriptures to Study

- Matthew 26:39
- John 4:34; 5:30; 6:21–38; 17:4
- Galatians 6:9

A Simple Prayer

Father, help us to guard and protect what You've entrusted to us. May our pursuit always be You first and foremost. Empower us to live Your design within our relationship and family. Cause us to be unified in purpose and to ferociously guard Your design for our marriage. Give us wisdom to know what we need to manage for, strength to uproot the things that we need to manage against, and the resolve to never settle for what's good at the expense of what is great.

Chapter 10

NOW WHAT?

A Timeless Truth
If you want a marriage that thrives, you must live with resolve and an ongoing intentionality to live purpose focused.

In his book *Think and Grow Rich,* Napoleon Hill tells a story of a great warrior who faced a battle against a powerful enemy. Though he and his men were outnumbered, the man sailed his soldiers into the enemy's country, and, after unloading all the soldiers, equipment, and supplies, gave the order to burn the ships. "Addressing his men before the first battle, he said, 'You see the boats going up in smoke. That means that we cannot leave these shores alive unless we win! We now have no choice—we win, or we perish!' They won."[1]

> A Thought from Zig Ziglar
> You were born to win, but to be a winner, you must plan to win, prepare to win, and expect to win.[2]

We want to ensure your marriage purpose succeeds and that the two of you win. So we need to hit you in the face with a little truth—but know we are smacking you with the utmost love. Well, at least Julie is; Greg kind of likes punching people with the truth. Either way, don't say we didn't warn you.

Knowing your purpose is good, but it's not good enough. Wanting to live God's purpose is a noble desire, but want-to and follow-through are entirely different. If you want a marriage that thrives, you must intentionally live purpose focused. Look at it this way. A person can want to lose weight, but their progress always involves a process. They need to make changes, commit to new habits, and then consistently follow through in doing what they know they should do. After all, growth takes time. New habits demand discipline, and living your marriage purpose requires your resolve and your intentionality.

As we've assisted couples in discovering their purpose, we've enjoyed the privilege of watching many of them overcome insurmountable odds to truly live purpose-focused lives together. At other times, we've watched couples begin with good intentions but eventually grow apart. The difference was in their resolve and an ongoing, purpose-focused intentionality.

Providing a Safe Harbor

Vivian, a vivacious, outgoing, and full-of-life sanguine threatened to throw in the towel after seventeen years of marriage to her husband, Sam, an engineer who preferred facts to feelings. They stood on the brink of divorce, ready to sign papers of dissolution. When challenged to give it one more try, they committed to serve one another instead of looking to be served and to live out God's purpose for their marriage. They focused on areas of common ground and reflected on how their differences prepared them to parent their growing children—the main passion they shared together. Instead of competing with one another, or operating with a mentality of my-way-is-better-than-yours, they contemplated how two are better than one.

Now, nearly a decade and a half later, Sam and Vivian fight for one another, not with one another. When Vivian received a diagnosis of cancer, Sam rallied around her with loving support. They battled together against selfishness, separation, and sickness—and they won! Together they live with a common vision to live out their marriage purpose of providing a safe harbor to all their kids' friends.

Making a Difference

Then there's Aiden and Abbey. Talk about a night-and-day different couple—Aiden and Abbey in many ways couldn't be more opposite of one another. Abbey takes care of all the needs of their home and homeschools their children. She loves serving at their church and in their local community. She's talkative, outgoing, and loves being involved with Girl Scouts and helping their children create projects. Abbey scrapbooks, bakes cookies, and loves family time. She has no ambition to travel the world or desire to be on the front line of running a business.

Aiden, on the other hand, loves making money. He buys houses and flips them for a profit. He never opens a scrapbook unless prompted, let alone puts one together. He loves his kids, but a 24/7 shift would cause a nervous breakdown. He's on the go, loves to travel to other countries, and finds a thrill impacting leaders in other nations.

When first married, Aiden and Abbey didn't even share the same faith. As our friendship grew, we encouraged them to identify how their differences made them stronger. Though they faced a lot of uphill battles, they resolved to work things out. When Aiden became a Christian, they determined to live toward God's purpose for their marriage.

Now, as Aiden buys and sells homes for a profit, Abbey loves supporting behind the scenes. She oversees details of all the accounts receivable and accounts payable for their company. They both agree their proceeds will be used to allow Abbey to stay at home with the kids and to support Aiden's calling of impacting other nations. They buy and flip homes as a family so they can give abundantly to God's kingdom. They each play their part and stay connected by their unified purpose of making a difference at home and abroad.

Building and Restoring What Others Cannot

Beth and Matt married late in life. Though separated by fifteen years in age, the two could not be more compatible. They didn't necessarily share the same rocky start as Aiden and Abbey or Sam and Vivian. But having both come from a divorced background, they recognized early in their relationship their need to live into God's purpose for their marriage. From the very beginning, they identified their common love for building and constructing homes. What began as weekend projects around the house evolved to volunteering their skills and time to undertake projects for their church. Eventually they traveled to other countries to build homes and schools and construct shelters for needy orphans. Today, nearly two decades later, they use their talents to take on projects others lack the ability to do. Each year they talk together to decide which project they will tackle for God. They plan vacation time around mission trips, and, when asked, respond by saying, "We're having more fun in our sixties than we did in our thirties. We're living God's purpose and loving life." They resolve and make great sacrifices to use their skills to build and restore what others cannot.

Though these couples live entirely different purposes, they are all resolved to fulfill God's plan for their marriages, both intentionally and consistently. It's not always easy. Living their marriage purpose requires deliberate thought and time for reflection—they constantly remind themselves of who God is and what He has promised. At times they recognized the need to realign their course to stay in line with God's plan, while at other times they realized the need to release their outcome and simply do the next right thing. At every turn, these couples chose to relish and celebrate the little moments of life that others often overlook.

> **A Thought from Bill Farrel**
> A man with a plan will always do better than a man who lives by accident.[3]

Steady yourselves, mates, as we reveal four final strategies to help you move forward with resolve. Let there be no retreat. Burn your ships and resolve to *fight for* and *live into* your marriage purpose. After all, every sailor worth his salt fights for what he believes in. Throughout the remaining pages of this book, we want to equip you with four proven strategies—remember God's promises, realign the vision when necessary, release the outcomes, and relish every moment—strategies Mary and Joseph embraced during Jesus' earliest years.

A Discovery from God's Word

> After Herod died, an angel of the Lord appeared in a dream to Joseph in Egypt and said, "Get up, take the child and his mother and go to the land of Israel, for those who were trying to take the child's life are dead."[4]

Joseph jumped from his bed and enthusiastically hugged Mary. "Mary, it's time. We can finally move closer to home."

Mary tilted her head slightly to the right and looked at Joseph inquisitively. "I don't understand," she said. "We just talked about this a couple days ago and you insisted we needed to stay in Egypt. Why the sudden change?"

Joseph smiled. "An angel appeared to me last night in a dream and told me to return to Israel. Mary, we can finally head back to Judea! We can finally raise Jesus where He was born—in Bethlehem."

Mary and Joseph embraced one another, excited to head closer to their old home. They missed their community. It wouldn't be easy to leave all they had acquired during their stay in Egypt, but the monetary loss would easily be compensated with the joy of familiarity and their closer proximity to family. Together, Joseph and Mary packed what little belongings they could and headed toward Judea. And then, just as it so often happens in our own lives, God changed their direction. Instead of heading to the land of Judea, God redirected them toward Galilee. Jesus would become a Nazarene.

Isn't that how life often happens? Sometimes as we journey toward our end destination, our direction and intention are redefined by the clarity we gain. Mary, Joseph, and Jesus still arrived safely in the land of Israel, but instead of their first suspected land of Judea and Bethlehem, God corrected their course toward Galilee.

THE QUESTION
How do we move forward from here?

Four Strategies to Move Forward

Along the way, God corrects all of our courses. After all, no couple ever knows in advance every step of their A–Z journey. As we intentionally reflect and realign our life to move toward God's purpose for our marriage, God faithfully corrects our course and helps us know what to do next, reminding us to remember who He is and to hold fast to what He has promised.

Strategy One: Remember God's Promise

As God directs our course, we must constantly remind ourselves of the purpose He promised and entrusted to us. Remembering Him empowers us to press on and maintain humility. Trials will come, our treasure will be threatened, but remembering who God is and holding fast to His promises empowers us to intentionally press on, avoiding discouragement and resisting fear.

> A Thought from Brother Lawrence
> *The difficulties of life do not have to be unbearable. It is the way we look at them—through faith or unbelief—that makes them seem so. We must be convinced that our Father is full of love for us and that He only permits trials to come our way for our own good.*[5]

In Deuteronomy, Moses addresses God's people and discloses an essential strategy to move forward in God's purpose, saying it was God

> who fed you in the wilderness with manna, which your fathers did not know, that He might humble you and that He might test you, to do you good in the end—then you say in your heart, "My power and the might of my hand have gained me this wealth." And you shall remember the Lord your God, for it is He who gives you power to get wealth, that He may establish His covenant which He swore to your fathers, as it is this day.[6]

Battles seem unconquerable when we focus on our circumstances. But when we remember whom we serve and focus on what He has promised, we are unstoppable. Nothing is impossible to those who back their vision with faith, regardless of the oppositions they face.

Remember Nehemiah and how he led God's people to do what others thought impossible? During those fifty-two days of rebuilding Judah's walls, they weren't without resistance. Many enemies tried to stop them. But guess what? Nehemiah leveraged the same strategy as Moses when he told the people, "Don't be afraid of them. Remember the Lord, who is great and awesome, and fight for your brothers, your sons and your daughters, your wives and your homes."[7]

And then there's David. When facing Goliath, David remembered who God was and all God could do. David said, "The Lord who delivered me from the paw of the lion and from the paw of the bear will deliver me from the hand of this Philistine."[8] All throughout the Psalms David sings the same strategy time and time again: "I will remember the deeds of the Lord; yes, I will remember your miracles of long ago."[9] "I remember the days of long ago; I meditate on all your works and consider what your hands have done."[10] "Many, O Lord my God, are the wonders you have done. The things you planned for us no one can recount to you; were I to speak and tell of them, they would be too many to declare."[11]

Don't miss this vital strategy. Moses, Nehemiah, David, and every other biblical example used throughout this book were living, breathing, everyday people like us. And they believed God.

AN INTENTIONAL APPLICATION

If you haven't done so already, post your marriage purpose in a place you'll visit often. Set aside time to connect and ensure you stay committed to that vision.

By remembering who God is and holding fast to what He has promised, God secures hope for us to humbly do all He designed us to do and realigns our vision with His perfect vision every day.

> **A Thought from Corrie ten Boom**
> *Never be afraid to trust an unknown future to a known God.*[12]

Strategy Two: Realign the Vision When Necessary

Earlier we shared about Joseph and Mary. They began their trip with the intention of landing in Bethlehem, but along the way God gave them additional clarity. Matthew Henry points out a powerful truth about their story that's applicable to our own journey of faith. He writes, "God could have given him these instructions with the former, but God reveals his mind to his people by degrees, to keep them still waiting on him, and expecting to hear further from him."[13]

Proverbs 3:5–6 ties in the necessity of remembering God and realigning the vision, when Solomon writes, "Trust in the Lord with all your heart and lean not on your own understanding; in all your ways acknowledge him, and he will make your paths straight." Solomon continues to share this vital strategy all throughout Proverbs, reminding us: "In his heart a man plans his course, but the Lord determines his steps,"[14] and "many are the plans in a man's heart, but it is the Lord's purpose that prevails."[15] The prophet Jeremiah reveals much the same in his prayers: "I know, O Lord, that a man's life is not his own; it is not for man to direct his steps."[16]

AN INTENTIONAL APPLICATION
Think from God's perspective today. What does He see as necessary changes you need to make in order to fully live into His design for your marriage?

Sometimes, in order to realign our purpose with God's, we need time for reflection in order to gain perspective. We've found it helpful to change up our routine to gain that perspective. Our friend Scott Fay often uses a beach ball to illustrate that the colors a person sees are determined by where they're sitting. Some see orange, yellow, or white, while others see green, red, or blue. The same exists in life. Sometimes we simply need to change our perspective, for, by changing our perspective, we see things differently and position ourselves to receive God's promises. We make sacrifices because our beliefs compel us to action.

How do we gain perspective? We do this by keeping our purpose in front of us, by remembering our why, and by remembering that vision fuels our purpose. So revisit your purpose statement often. Use it to serve as a beacon for your direction. Ask yourselves: What areas do we need to change to produce optimal results?

Sometimes people read a book and then never look at it again. Don't do that with this book! We encourage you to frequently revisit and discuss again your findings. What's the same and what has changed? By doing so, you generate time for reflection and the opportunity to realign your thoughts with God's purpose.

Realigning our thoughts with God's inspires within us faith to believe that He will provide all He has promised. He does what we cannot. And He alone is God, pointing us to the third vital strategy to successfully live out God's purpose for our marriage.

A Thought from Pam Farrel
Success is doing your very best and leaving the result to God.[17]

Strategy Three: Release the Outcome

At some point in your journey, your marriage purpose will be challenged. Sometimes the Enemy tells us that what we do isn't good enough and compares it against another's value. Paul reminds the church in Corinth, concerning his and Apollos' works that "neither the one who plants nor the one who waters is anything, but only God, who makes things grow."[18]

God alone causes growth to take place. Of course we must live responsible, dependable, and even accountable to God for living out His purpose, but at some point in our journey we must release our outcome to Him. Taking too much responsibility may mean we've forgotten to remember that God is God—we aren't. We will answer to Him concerning our faithfulness, but we will not be held accountable for the results of our faithfulness.

AN INTROSPECTIVE CHALLENGE
God doesn't call us to be successful;
He calls us to be obedient.

Shadrach, Meshach, and Abednego understood this vital truth of fulfilling God's purpose for their lives. Abandoned to God's vision and committed to doing the right thing, they released their outcome to God by telling Nebuchadnezzar, "We do not need to defend ourselves before you in this matter. If we are thrown into the blazing furnace, the God we serve is able to save us from it, and he will rescue us from your hand, O king. But even if he does not, we want you to know, O king, that we will not serve your gods or worship the image of gold you have set up."[19]

Do you see their resolve? Did you capture how they released the outcome to the Lord? They believed God could deliver them from the fiery furnace, but even if He didn't, they determined never to bow down to any other god but the Lord. They remained faithful right where they were.

AN INTENTIONAL APPLICATION
In what ways you have stopped moving forward, allowing your *how* to get in the way of your *what*?

Releasing the outcome doesn't diminish our need for intentionality; instead, it liberates us to simply be faithful. Remember our mailer story? By releasing the outcome to God, we better celebrate and relish every moment along our journey. Concerning our lives with the outcome distracts us from the joy of our journey—this may be one of the most difficult lessons for us to learn. When we get tied up in the outcomes, it stops us. When we get too busy doing *for* God, we forget the joy of being *with* Him.

Do you remember the story of Mary and Martha? When Mary and Martha prepared for Jesus and His disciples, Martha became distracted by activity. Her task became laborious. She began resenting Mary, who didn't seem to be working as hard. Come on now, you know you can relate. Haven't you ever gotten to the point where doing for God lost its luster and you wanted to blame someone else? When that happens, it's time to reprioritize so we can relish life again by:

1. Remembering who God is. Sometimes we may be jealous or frustrated; somewhere we get off track with our motives and feel shortchanged. We become disgruntled and unmotivated. These are usually telltale signs that we need to feed our spirit to overcome our more fleshly tendencies.

2. Hold fast to what He's promised. Sometimes we get discouraged or weary. We want more, we want greater results, but we can't see how we are ever going to do what we desire. The solution is to remember that God will never leave us until He fulfills *all* that He has promised.[20]

3. Release the outcome. We aren't in charge of the outcome—God is. He can do whatever He wants. He is God and we are not. We simply need to be faithful, to live for

His approval (not other people's), to live for His pleasure, and to make Him known.

Strategy Four: Relish Every Moment

Jesus looked at Martha who complained that He should make Mary help, by saying, "Martha, Martha…you are worried and upset about many things, but only one thing is needed. Mary has chosen what is better, and it will not be taken away from her."[21] The temptation of living purpose focused transpires as we busy our lives with too much activity. Instead, God reminds us to relish the life He's given to us as a couple.

AN INTROSPECTIVE CHALLENGE
Every morning ask God,
*What do You want us to focus on and
how can we best serve You today?*

We learned this principle of relishing every moment in life within the first three years of our marriage. Julie was pregnant with our second child, and well into her last trimester. It was hot in Missouri, and like many women in their last trimester, Julie wasn't getting a lot of sleep. Her feet were swollen, her hands were swollen, she was swollen, and well, she was ready to not be pregnant.

At seven and a half months, the thought occurred to her: *Embrace the process. Relish every moment of this time. Enjoy every kick. This will be the last time you feel life within you.* It completely changed everything. She realized a premature birth would not deliver optimal results, so she began to appreciate the process, understanding it would be the last time she experienced the privilege of bearing a child. Instead of agonizing the last nine weeks of pregnancy, Julie savored every kick; she enjoyed every time a woman touched her belly and said, "You're beautiful."

AN INTENTIONAL APPLICATION
Talk together about the ways you can better relish every moment of life.

To truly live in the life God entrusted to you and your spouse, you'll need to press toward your future while fully embracing your current circumstances. So remember whom you serve. Realign your vision as necessary, release your outcome, and relish every moment of life. Keep your vision and your purpose in front of you to serve as a litmus test and a guide for what to say yes to and what to say no to.

Two Are Better Than One

Well, there you have it. You've discovered your secret treasure. You hold next-step actions to living it out and a plan to sustain it. We hope you'll take a moment to connect with us. We'd love to hear your story and what you discovered while reading *Two Are Better Than One: Buid Purpose and Unity in Your Marriage*. If you'd like to take a deeper dive into your purpose and learn more about scheduling your own personal two-day Marriage Reboot Retreat for you and your spouse, visit https://marriedforapurpose.com/reboot-marriage-retreat/.

We'd love for you to connect with us on Facebook by visiting our page at www.facebook.com/marriedforapurpose, where you'll receive daily thoughts to strengthen your relationship and move you toward fulfilling your marriage purpose. And finally, we hope you'll take a little more time to connect with one another by answering the following questions in this final chapter study guide.

Study Guide: Chapter 10

Questions to Consider

1. What creative ways can you continue to inspire God's purpose for your marriage? (Post your purpose statement in a place you will see it often, revisit the charts you completed in this book, etc.)

2. Periodically talk together to evaluate if any part of your vision needs to be realigned. If you feel a little sideways, ask one another: What's the next step (not the next ten, just the next step) that we need to take to move toward God's purpose?

3. Establish times to connect at the beginning of your day, and take time for reflection at the end of your day. Ask questions like: How can we add value to one another? How can we add value to others? What kind of atmosphere are we providing in our home? Are the activities we are participating in still important? Has anything changed? How can we best live God's purpose for our marriage during this season of life?

4. How does the statement, "God doesn't call us to be successful; He calls us to be obedient," encourage you as a couple? In what ways are you being faithful right where you are?

5. How can you better stay connected and relish every moment of life together? Take a moment to schedule

time to enjoy life more fully by putting the following thoughts on your calendar:

- How can I wow my spouse today?
- How can I make my spouse laugh?
- How can I flirt with my spouse today?

6. How has reading this book changed your lives?
7. How will knowing your purpose inspire life going forward?

Scriptures to Study

- Deuteronomy 8:17–18
- 1 Samuel 17:37
- Nehemiah 4:14
- Psalm 40:5; 77:11; 143:5
- Proverbs 16:9; 19:21
- Jeremiah 10:23
- Daniel 3:16–18
- Luke 10:41–42
- 1 Corinthians 3:7

Remember that stress fades as we release the outcome and our illusion of control to God. Pray together. Seek Him daily as a couple.

A Simple Prayer

Father, thank You for entrusting such a special vision to us. Help us to always remember You and the promises You've whispered throughout this process. Help us to truly live out Your vision for our marriage. If we get off course, help us to realign our lives to Your perfect plan. Never allow us to hold back because of fear or run ahead of You out of ambition. Instead, help us walk hand in hand with one another, faithfully releasing all the results and outcomes of our life to You. Thank You for loving us. Help us to honor You by keeping You first in everything and relishing the life You've given us together. Amen.

ABOUT THE AUTHORS

GREG AND JULIE GORMAN, authors of *What I Wish My Mother Had Told Me About Marriage* and *Married for a Purpose* have been teaching biblical truths for marriage for nearly two decades. They are the founders of Married for a Purpose, a faith-based organization committed to providing life-transforming content and pathways to sustainable growth. Together they write, produce, and host weekly broadcasts, and are certified by Dr. John C. Maxwell as executive coaches and trainers. Greg and Julie empower believers to discover God's fingerprint design for their lives and assist married couples to discover the purpose God has for their marriage. They, along with their three children, make their home in southern Florida.

If you would like to learn more about them or if you'd like to get in touch with Greg and Julie, you can visit them at MarriedforaPurpose.com.

ENDNOTES

Chapter 1: What's the Big Idea?
1. Isaiah 46:10–11.
2. Rick Warren, *The Purpose Driven Life* (Grand Rapids, MI: Zondervan, 2014), 235.
3. Genesis 1:28.
4. Paraphrased from Genesis 1:29.
5. Genesis 1:26.
6. v. 28.
7. 28:15.
8. James 1:5.
9. Jeremiah 29:11.
10. 2 Chronicles 16:9.
11. Aristotle, accessed December 7, 2015, http://www.goodreads.com/quotes/20103-the-whole-is-greater-than-the-sum-of-its-parts.
12. Matthew 18:19.
13. v. 20.
14. Galatians 5:15, NKJV.
15. Mother Teresa, accessed December 7, 2015, http://www.goodreads.com/quotes/63168-i-can-do-things-you-cannot-you-can-do-things.
16. Mark 6:7.
17. Ephesians 2:10.
18. 2 Peter 1:3.
19. Romans 12:6.
20. Matthew 19:5.
21. v. 6.
22. Ecclesiastes 4:9–12.
23. Deuteronomy 32:30.
24. Stephen Arterburn, *Regret-Free Living: Hope for Past Mistakes and Freedom from Unhealthy Patterns,* accessed December 7, 2015, http://www.goodreads.com/work/quotes/6889586-regret-free-living-hope-for-past-mistakes-and-freedom-from-unhealthy-pa.
25. Visit www.MarriedforaPurpose.com for additional resources.

Chapter 2: Are There Clues?

1. A paraphrased quote from the 1964 to 1973 TV series *Underdog*.
2. Andy Stanley, accessed December 7, 2015, https://www.goodreads.com/quotes/556851-direction-not-intention-determines-your-destination.
3. Nehemiah 2:20.
4. v. 5.
5. v. 6.
6. Matthew 7:24–25.
7. R. A. Torrey, *The Power of Prayer* (New Kensington, PA: Whitaker House, 2000), 15.
8. Matthew 5:16.
9. Matthew 28:19; Mark 16:15; Luke 24:47–48.
10. John 15:16.
11. 20:21.
12. Rick Warren, *The Purpose Driven Life*, 17.
13. Tom Paterson, *Living the Life You Were Meant to Live* (Littleton, CO: PatersonCenter, 2002), Introduction.
14. Bill and Pam Farrel, *The Secret Language of Successful Couples* (Eugene, OR: Harvest House, 2009), 51.
15. Matthew 10:3.
16. 4:18–20.
17. 11:25.
18. Ephesians 4:8–13.
19. Romans 12:6–8.
20. Matthew 5:14–16.
21. Revelation 4:11; Colossians 1:16.
22. Brother Lawrence, *The Practice of the Presence* (New Kensington, PA: Whitaker House, 1982), 48.
23. Eric, Liddell, accessed December 7, 2015, https://www.goodreads.com/author/quotes/802465.Eric_Liddell.
24. Romans 11:36.
25. Philippians 2:1–4.
26. Dale Carnegie, accessed December 7, 2015, http://www.goodreads.com/author/quotes/3317.Dale_Carnegie.
27. Stephen Arterburn, *Regret-Free Living*.
28. John 13:34; 15:12.
29. Lance Witt, *Replenish* (Grand Rapids, MI: Baker Books, 2011), 109.
30. Ephesians 5:31–32.
31. Revelation 19:7.
32. Shannon and Greg Ethridge, *Every Woman's Marriage* (Colorado Springs, CO: Waterbrook Press, 2006), 38.

Chapter 3: Do You Live Problem Focused or Purpose Focused?

1. Paraphrased from Proverbs 23:7.
2. Napoleon Hill, *Think and Grow Rich* (Radford, VA: Wilder Publications, 2007), 43.
3. Jim Collins, *Good to Great* (New York, NY: HarperCollins, 2001), 9.
4. Ibid., 11.
5. 1 Samuel 17:45.
6. Paraphrased from 1 Samuel 17:25.
7. 1 Samuel 17:45, NKJV.
8. John C. Maxwell, *Think on These Things* (Kansas City, MO: Beacon Hill Press, 1999), 9.
9. Romans 12:1.
10. Ephesians 4:22–24.
11. Philippians 4:8.
12. 2 Timothy 1:7.
13. 2 Corinthians 10:5–6.
14. 2 Peter 1:3.
15. Stephen R. Covey, *The 7 Habits of Highly Effective People: Powerful Lessons in Personal Change* (New York, NY: Free Press, 2004), 28.
16. Quoted in Bruce and Darlene Marie Wilkinson, *The Dream Giver for Parents* (Sisters, OR: Multnomah Publishers, 2004), 43.
17. Romans 8:28.
18. Maxwell, *Think on These Things*, 13.
19. John 10:10.
20. Aristotle, accessed December 7, 2015, http://www.goodreads.com/quotes/603119-we-are-what-we-repeatedly-do-greatness-then-is-not.
21. Matthew 18:19–20.

Chapter 4: How Does God Confirm His Purpose?

1. Genesis 12:1–2.
2. Ibid.
3. Winston Churchill, accessed December 7, 2015, https://www.goodreads.com/author/quotes/2834066.Winston_Churchill.
4. Warren, *The Purpose Driven Life*, 20.
5. Isaiah 45:1.
6. v. 2.
7. v. 13.
8. Psalm 119:105.
9. John Ruskin, accessed December 7, 2015, https://www.goodreads.com/author/quotes/1606.John_Ruskin.
10. 2 Chronicles 16:9.

11 Psalm 23:3; Isaiah 40:29.
12 Romans 8:28.
13 2 Timothy 3:16.
14 Philippians 4:7.
15 Luke 1:41.
16 Matthew 1:20; 2:12–13, 19, 22.
17 Judges 6:36–40.
18 Exodus 4:3–4.
19 Jeremiah 29:13.
20 1 Samuel 16:18.
21 Matthew 2:10–11.
22 Genesis 20:14–16.
23 Warren, *The Purpose Driven Life*, 250.

Chapter 5: Why Are We So Different?
1 Mark 3:24–25.
2 1 Chronicles 15:29.
3 2 Samuel 6:20.
4 v. 21–22.
5 v. 23.
6 Andrew Carnegie, accessed December 8, 2015, https://www.goodreads.com/author/quotes/23387.Andrew_Carnegie.
7 Robert A. Rohm, *Positive Personality Profiles* (Atlanta, GA: Personality Insights Press, 2014), 16.
8 Proverbs 27:17.
9 Phillip Wagner, *The Marriage Makeover* (Franklin, TN: Authentic, 2013), 50.
10 Malcolm Forbes, accessed December 8, 2015, http://www.brainyquote.com/quotes/quotes/m/malcolmfor151513.html.
11 Tom Rath and Barry Conchie, *Strengths Based Leadership* (New York, NY: Gallup Press, 2008), 22.
12 Drs. Les and Leslie Parrott, *Relationships* (Grand Rapids, MI: Zondervan, 1998), 67.
13 Romans 14:1, 3.
14 Paterson, *Living the Life You Were Meant to Live*, 12.
15 1 Corinthians 12:12–14.
16 v. 15–18.

Chapter 6: What's Our Common Ground?
1 Abraham Lincoln, "House Divided Speech," accessed December 8, 2015, http://www.abrahamlincolnonline.org/lincoln/speeches/house.htm.
2 Ibid. See also Luke 11:17.

3 Romans 16:3–4.
4 Acts 18:26.
5 1 Corinthians 16:19–20.
6 Acts 18:18.
7 Romans 16:3–4.
8 Les and Leslie Parrott, "How to Predict a Happy Marriage," accessed December 8, 2015, http://www.lesandleslie.com/devotions/how-to-predict-a-happy-marriage/.
9 Acts 2:42.
10 v. 44.
11 v. 47.
12 For more information, visit www.tablegroup.com.
13 Paterson, *Living the Life You Were Meant to Live*, 7.
14 Hill, *Think and Grow Rich*, 69.
15 Paterson, *Living the Life You Were Meant to Live*, 21.
16 L. P. Jacks, *Education through Recreation* (New York, NY: Harper & Brothers, 1932), 1.
17 T. D. Jakes, accessed December 8, 2015, http://www.goodreads.com/quotes/636989-if-you-can-t-figure-out-your-purpose-figure-out-your.

Chapter 7: What Fuels Our Purpose?

1 Stephen Covey, Wikipedia article, "*The 7 Habits of Highly Effective People*," accessed December 8, 2015, https://en.wikipedia.org/wiki/The_7_Habits_of_Highly_Effective_People.
2 Isaiah 55:8–9.
3 Romans 8:11.
4 Psalm 32:8; John 14:26.
5 1 Corinthians 2:16.
6 Psalm 37:4.
7 Genesis 39:23.
8 Paraphrased from Genesis 37:9.
9 Genesis 37:10.
10 v. 19–20.
11 John C. Maxwell, *Intentional Living* (New York, NY: Center Street Hachette Book Group, 2015), 259.
12 Warren, *The Purpose Driven Life*, 220.
13 Proverbs 22:6.
14 Lawrence, *The Practice of the Presence*, 24.
15 John C. Maxwell, *Put Your Dream to the Test* (Nashville, TN: Thomas Nelson, 2009), 38.

16 Jim Loehr and Tony Schwartz, *The Power of Full Engagement* (New York, NY: The Free Press, 2005), 13.
17 Ibid.
18 Psalm 139:15–16.
19 Jeremiah 1:5.
20 Matthew 6:9–10.
21 Hill, *Think and Grow Rich*, 32.
22 T. E. Lawrence, Wikipedia article, "T. E. Lawrence," accessed December 8, 2015, https://en.wikiquote.org/wiki/T._E._Lawrence.
23 Maxwell, *Put Your Dream to the Test*, 41.

Chapter 8: How Do We Define Our Purpose?

1 John C. Maxwell, accessed December 8, 2015, http://www.brainyquote.com/quotes/quotes/j/johncmaxw163254.html.
2 Habakkuk 2:2–3.
3 v. 2.
4 Jeremiah 30:2.
5 Isaiah 49:16.
6 Jim Collins, *Good to Great*, 1.
7 Ibid.

Chapter 9: How Do We Protect God's Purpose?

1 W. Clement Stone, accessed December 8, 2015, http://www.brainyquote.com/quotes/quotes/w/wclements193782.html.
2 Hebrews 12:2–3.
3 John 6:26–28.
4 v. 38.
5 5:30.
6 17:4.
7 Luke 9:51.
8 Alan Lakein, accessed December 8, 2015, http://www.goodreads.com/quotes/15737-failing-to-plan-is-planning-to-fail.
9 Scott M. Fay, *Discover Your Sweet Spot* (New York, NY: Morgan James Publishing, 2014), 14.
10 Galatians 6:9.
11 Fay, *Discover Your Sweet Spot*, 47.
12 Stephen Covey, accessed December 8, 2015, https://www.goodreads.com/author/quotes/1538.Stephen_R_Covey.
13 Developed by Paterson and Richardson, *LifePlan: The Art of Facilitating LifePlans*, 94.

Chapter 10: Now What?

1. Hill, *Think and Grow Rich*, 26.
2. Zig Ziglar, accessed December 8, 2015, http://www.brainyquote.com/quotes/authors/z/zig_ziglar.html.
3. Bill Farrel, *7 Simple Skills for Every Man* (Eugene, OR: Harvest House, 2014), 51.
4. Matthew 2:19–20.
5. Brother Lawrence, *The Practice of the Presence* (New Kensington, PA: Whitaker House, 1982), 55.
6. Deuteronomy 8:16–18, NKJV.
7. Nehemiah 4:14.
8. 1 Samuel 17:37.
9. Psalm 77:11.
10. 143:5.
11. 40:5.
12. Corrie ten Boom, accessed December 8, 2015, http://www.goodreads.com/quotes/70125-never-be-afraid-to-trust-an-unknown-future-to-a.
13. Matthew Henry's Commentary on the Whole Bible: New Modern Edition, Electronic Database. Copyright © 1991 by Hendrickson Publishers, Inc.
14. Proverbs 16:9.
15. 19:21.
16. Jeremiah 10:23.
17. Pam Farrel, *7 Simple Skills for Every Woman* (Eugene, OR: Harvest House, 2015), 81.
18. 1 Corinthians 3:7.
19. Daniel 3:16–18.
20. Genesis 28:15.
21. Luke 10:41–42.

MarriedforaPurpose.com

www.ingramcontent.com/pod-product-compliance
Lightning Source LLC
Chambersburg PA
CBHW050905160426
43194CB00011B/2290